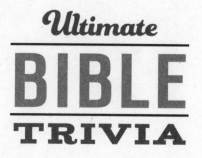

Ultimate

BIBLE

TRIVIA

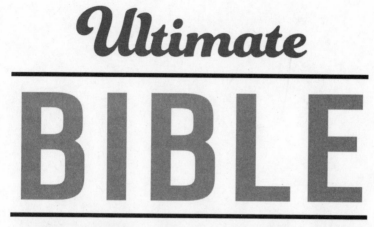

Ultimate BIBLE TRIVIA

**Questions, Puzzles, and Quizzes
from Genesis to Revelation**

TIMOTHY E. PARKER

Revell
a division of Baker Publishing Group
Grand Rapids, Michigan

© 2016 by Timothy E. Parker

Published by Revell
a division of Baker Publishing Group
PO Box 6287, Grand Rapids, MI 49516-6287
www.revellbooks.com

Repackaged edition published 2019
ISBN 978-0-8007-3674-3

Printed in the United States of America

The Library of Congress has cataloged the original edition as follows:
Names: Parker, Timothy E., author.
Title: The official Bible brilliant trivia book : questions, puzzles, and quizzes from
    Genesis to Revelation / Timothy E. Parker.
Description: Grand Rapids : Revell, 2016. | Includes bibliographical references.
Identifiers: LCCN 2016011272 | ISBN 9780800727062 (pbk.)
Subjects: LCSH: Bible—Miscellanea. | Bible games and puzzles.
Classification: LCC BS612 .P28 2016 | DDC 220—dc23
LC record available at http://lccn.loc.gov/2016011272

Scripture quotations are from the King James Version of the Bible.

23   24   25   7

To all those seeking a deeper relationship
with Jesus Christ, the one true God

CONTENTS

Specialized Multiple-Choice Trivia 111

Scripture Fill in the Blanks 155

SECTION 2: THE INTERMEDIATE SECTION

Specialized True or False Trivia 179

Word Searches 191

SECTION 3: THE BONUS SECTION

BEFORE YOU BEGIN

Joshua 1:8 states, "This book of the law shall not depart out of thy mouth; but thou shalt meditate therein day and night, that thou mayest observe to do according to all that is written therein: for then thou shalt make thy way prosperous, and then thou shalt have good success." Although this book uses clever games, wordplay, and trivia to increase your overall Bible knowledge, its goal is no trivial matter. It behooves every believer to know as much about the Lord and his Word as humanly possible. This book will be overwhelmingly helpful in that endeavor.

To get the true benefits of this book, you may have to go through it more than once. The goal is to challenge you in multiple ways, using multiple strategies and a wide array of exercises, puzzles, and quizzes, to get you to the highest level of Bible knowledge. After you complete this volume of trivia questions, you'll be ready for the challenges in volume 2.

There is no penalty for doing the same exercise repeatedly until you feel comfortable and competent with it. This is not a race given to the swift; the victory will come to those who endure to the end. Feel free to do any exercise any number of times and record only your highest score.

It is far more important for you to learn and know the information in the exercises than to complete the exercises quickly. In fact, I strongly recommend that you never time yourself in any challenge presented but take your time and focus on retaining correct answers.

This is an open-book book. That means you may use your own Bible to find answers. It is always a good thing to have the Good Book open, and you are never penalized in any way for referencing your own Bible as you seek answers to the thousands of questions presented.

Some of the exercises may be easy for you, and some are maddeningly difficult. However, they all have one purpose, and that is to teach the Word of God and bring you to the highest levels of Bible understanding and true knowledge.

SECTION 1

THE MUST-KNOW SECTION

This section deals with Bible information, facts, and questions and answers that you absolutely must know to become Bible brilliant. (Answers to section 1 begin on page 215.)

> All human discoveries seem to be made only for the purpose of confirming more and more strongly the truths contained in the sacred Scriptures.
>
> Sir William Herschel

1 Do Not Be Fooled

This is a simple true or false test to get things started. Award yourself 10 points for each correct true or false answer. Complete the entire test before checking your answers.

1. _____ The phrase "This too shall pass" is in the Bible.

2. _____ Eve bit into the forbidden apple in the Garden of Eden.

3. _____ "Spare the rod, spoil the child" is a biblical teaching on child raising.

4. _____ "God works in mysterious ways" is from the book of Proverbs.

5. _____ One of the most-quoted Bible verses is "Cleanliness is next to godliness."

6. _____ Three wise men visited Jesus on the day of his birth.

7. _____ "The Little Drummer Boy" Christmas song is based on the boy drummer in Micah.

8. _____ According to the book that bears his name, Jonah was in the belly of a whale for three days and three nights.

9. _____ Satan took the form of a serpent when he tempted Eve in the garden of Eden.

10. _____ "God helps those who help themselves" is in the book of Psalms.

11. _____ "Money is the root of all evil" is a classic Bible verse concerning placing money above God.

12. _____ Jesus Christ himself said, "To thine own self be true."

13. _____ The apostle Paul said, "Love the sinner, hate the sin."

14. _____ The wise men visited the baby Jesus in the manger.

15. _____ There was one set of the Ten Commandments given to Moses.

2 The Essentials

To be truly Bible brilliant, you must have a strong, fundamental knowledge of the basics of the Bible. You may retake the following quiz as often as necessary. You earn 2 points per correct answer.

1. What is the Bible's very first verse?
2. Who was the mother of Jesus?
3. What garden was the home of Adam and Eve?
4. What type of creature tricked Eve into eating forbidden fruit?
5. What was the method of execution the Romans used to kill Jesus?
6. What are the wages of sin, according to the Bible?
7. What was the name of Moses's brother?
8. What crime did Cain commit?
9. Who was thrown into a den of lions?
10. Man was made in whose image?
11. How does the Lord's Prayer start?
12. What did Jesus use to feed five thousand people?
13. What part of Adam's body did God use to create Eve?
14. What is the only sin that cannot be forgiven?
15. From what substance did God create man?
16. The ark was built to save humankind from what disaster?
17. When accused of knowing Jesus, who denied him three times?
18. What was placed on the head of Jesus Christ before his crucifixion?
19. Who lied to God when questioned about the whereabouts of his brother?

20. The Ten Commandments were written on what material?

21. How many apostles followed Jesus?

22. Who was directed by an angel to go see the baby Jesus?

23. What is the second book of the Bible?

24. Before David became king, what was his occupation?

25. What is the first book of the Bible?

26. What is the first book of the New Testament?

27. How did David kill Goliath?

28. Where was the "wilderness" in which John the Baptist preached?

29. What was written at the top of Jesus's cross?

30. In what did Jesus sleep after his birth?

31. Who was willing to offer his son as a sacrifice to the Lord?

32. What was miraculous about Jesus's mother?

33. After Noah built the ark, for how many days and nights did it rain?

34. Who was placed in an ark of bulrushes and placed in a river by his mother?

35. What curious thing happened to Jonah?

36. How was Ruth related to Naomi?

37. To whom was Mary engaged when she became pregnant with Jesus?

38. What book of the Bible contains hymns written by David?

39. What animals drowned themselves in the sea when demons cast out by Jesus entered them?

40. What psalm begins, "The LORD is my shepherd"?

41. Who wrote the majority of the letters that form a large part of the New Testament?

42. What wicked things did Joseph's brothers do to him and to get rid of him?

43. Who was the father of King David?
44. Who was the father of Solomon?
45. What is the final book of the Bible?
46. What is the last word of the Bible?
47. How many individual books are in the Bible?
48. What humble act did Jesus do for his disciples at the Last Supper?
49. What was the name of Adam and Eve's first son?
50. How long did it take the Lord to make the heaven and the earth?

3 Books of the Bible

The following exercise will help you learn the precise order of all sixty-six books of the Holy Scriptures without fail. For each question, simply fill in the name of the Bible book in its proper place in the list.

After mastering this exercise, which may take several attempts, you will know not only the precise order of the books as they appear in the Bible but also such facts as the twentieth book is Proverbs and the forty-fifth book is Romans.

You will be filling in 186 various blanks for the sixty-six Bible books during this exercise. Award yourself 1 point per blank. You may do this exercise as many times as necessary and record only your best score.

1.

1. Genesis
2.

3. Leviticus
4.
5. Deuteronomy

2.

1.
2. Exodus
3. Leviticus
4. Numbers
5.

3.

1. Genesis
2. Exodus
3.
4. Numbers
5.

4.

1. Genesis
2.
3.
4. Numbers
5. Deuteronomy

5.

3. Leviticus
4.
5. Deuteronomy
6.
7. Judges
8. Ruth

6.

4. Numbers
5.
6. Joshua
7.
8.
9. 1 Samuel
10. 2 Samuel

7.

4. Numbers
5. Deuteronomy
6. Joshua
7.
8. Ruth
9.
10. 2 Samuel

8.

4. Numbers
5.
6. Joshua
7. Judges
8.
9. 1 Samuel
10.

9.

4. Numbers
5. Deuteronomy
6.

7. Judges
8.
9. 1 Samuel
10. 2 Samuel

10.

7. Judges
8.
9. 1 Samuel
10.
11. 1 Kings
12.
13. 1 Chronicles

11.

7. Judges
8. Ruth
9.
10. 2 Samuel
11.
12. 2 Kings
13.

12.

7. Judges
8. Ruth
9. 1 Samuel
10.
11. 1 Kings
12.
13. 1 Chronicles

13.

    7. Judges

    8.

    9. 1 Samuel

    10. 2 Samuel

    11.

    12. 2 Kings

    13.

14.

    11. 1 Kings

    12.

    13. 1 Chronicles

    14. 2 Chronicles

    15.

    16. Nehemiah

    17. Esther

    18.

    19. Psalms

    20. Proverbs

15.

    11. 1 Kings

    12. 2 Kings

    13. 1 Chronicles

    14. 2 Chronicles

    15.

    16. Nehemiah

    17.

    18. Job

    19.

    20. Proverbs

16.

11. 1 Kings
12. 2 Kings
13. 1 Chronicles
14. 2 Chronicles
15. Ezra
16.
17. Esther
18. Job
19. Psalms
20.

17.

11. 1 Kings
12. 2 Kings
13. 1 Chronicles
14. 2 Chronicles
15.
16. Nehemiah
17. Esther
18.
19. Psalms
20.

18.

11. 1 Kings
12.
13. 1 Chronicles
14. 2 Chronicles
15.
16. Nehemiah

17.
18. Job
19. Psalms
20.

19.

11.
12. 2 Kings
13. 1 Chronicles
14. 2 Chronicles
15. Ezra
16.
17. Esther
18. Job
19.
20. Proverbs

20.

17.
18. Job
19. Psalms
20.
21. Ecclesiastes
22.
23. Isaiah
24. Jeremiah
25. Lamentations

21.

17. Esther
18. Job

19.

20. Proverbs

21.

22. Song of Solomon

23.

24. Jeremiah

25. Lamentations

22.

17.

18. Job

19. Psalms

20. Proverbs

21.

22. Song of Solomon

23. Isaiah

24.

25. Lamentations

23.

17. Esther

18.

19. Psalms

20. Proverbs

21. Ecclesiastes

22.

23. Isaiah

24. Jeremiah

25.

24.

    20.

    21. Ecclesiastes

    22.

    23. Isaiah

    24. Jeremiah

    25. Lamentations

    26.

    27. Daniel

    28. Hosea

    29.

    30. Amos

25.

    20. Proverbs

    21. Ecclesiastes

    22.

    23. Isaiah

    24. Jeremiah

    25.

    26. Ezekiel

    27. Daniel

    28. Hosea

    29. Joel

    30.

26.

    20. Proverbs

    21. Ecclesiastes

    22. Song of Solomon

    23.

24. Jeremiah
25. Lamentations
26.
27. Daniel
28.
29. Joel
30. Amos

27.

20.
21. Ecclesiastes
22. Song of Solomon
23. Isaiah
24.
25. Lamentations
26. Ezekiel
27.
28. Hosea
29. Joel
30.

28.

20. Proverbs
21. Ecclesiastes
22.
23. Isaiah
24. Jeremiah
25.
26. Ezekiel
27. Daniel
28. Hosea

29.
30. Amos

29.

20. Proverbs
21. Ecclesiastes
22. Song of Solomon
23.
24. Jeremiah
25. Lamentations
26.
27.
28. Hosea
29.
30. Amos

30.

20.
21. Ecclesiastes
22. Song of Solomon
23. Isaiah
24.
25. Lamentations
26. Ezekiel
27.
28. Hosea
29. Joel
30.

31.

26.
27. Daniel

28. Hosea
29.
30. Amos
31. Obadiah
32.
33. Micah
34.
35. Habakkuk

32.

26. Ezekiel
27. Daniel
28.
29. Joel
30. Amos
31.
32. Jonah
33.
34. Nahum
35. Habakkuk

33.

26.
27. Daniel
28. Hosea
29. Joel
30. Amos
31.
32. Jonah
33. Micah
34.
35. Habakkuk

34.

   26. Ezekiel

   27.

   28. Hosea

   29. Joel

   30. Amos

   31. Obadiah

   32.

   33. Micah

   34. Nahum

   35.

35.

   30. Amos

   31. Obadiah

   32.

   33. Micah

   34. Nahum

   35.

   36. Zephaniah

   37.

   38. Zechariah

   39. Malachi

36.

   30. Amos

   31. Obadiah

   32. Jonah

   33.

   34. Nahum

   35. Habakkuk

36.
37. Haggai
38. Zechariah
39.

37.

30. Amos
31.
32. Jonah
33. Micah
34.
35. Habakkuk
36. Zephaniah
37.
38. Zechariah
39.

38.

30. Amos
31. Obadiah
32.
33. Micah
34. Nahum
35.
36. Zephaniah
37.
38. Zechariah
39. Malachi

39.

30.
31. Obadiah

32. Jonah
33.
34. Nahum
35. Habakkuk
36.
37. Haggai
38.
39. Malachi

Fill in each of the twenty-seven books of the New Testament as necessary to create a perfect order.

40.

40. Matthew
41. Mark
42.
43. John
44. Acts (of the Apostles)

41.

40.
41. Mark
42. Luke
43.
44. Acts

42.

40. Matthew
41.
42. Luke
43. John
44.

43.

40. Matthew
41.
42. Luke
43.
44. Acts
45.
46.
47.
48. Galatians
49.
50. Philippians
51. Colossians
52. 1 Thessalonians

44.

43. John
44.
45. Romans
46. 1 Corinthians
47.
48. Galatians
49. Ephesians
50.

45.

43.
44.
45. Romans
46.
47. 2 Corinthians

48.
49. Ephesians
50. Philippians

46.

43. John
44. Acts
45.
46. 1 Corinthians
47. 2 Corinthians
48.
49. Ephesians
50. Philippians
51.
52. 1 Thessalonians
53.

47.

47.
48. Galatians
49.
50. Philippians
51.
52. 1 Thessalonians
53. 2 Thessalonians
54. 1 Timothy
55.
56. Titus

48.

49. Ephesians
50.

51. Colossians

52.

53. 2 Thessalonians

49.

49.

50. Philippians

51.

52. 1 Thessalonians

53. 2 Thessalonians

54. 1 Timothy

55. 2 Timothy

56.

57. Philemon

58.

59. James

50.

49. Ephesians

50.

51. Colossians

52. 1 Thessalonians

53.

54. 1 Timothy

55. 2 Timothy

56. Titus

57.

58. Hebrews

59.

51.

49.

50. Philippians

51. Colossians

52. 1 Thessalonians

53. 2 Thessalonians

54.

55.

56. Titus

57.

58. Hebrews

59.

52.

50.

51.

52. 1 Thessalonians

53. 2 Thessalonians

54. 1 Timothy

55. 2 Timothy

56.

57. Philemon

58. Hebrews

59.

60. 1 Peter

53.

53.

54. 1 Timothy

55. 2 Timothy

56. Titus

57.

58. Hebrews

59. James

60.

54.

50. Philippians

51. Colossians

52. 1 Thessalonians

53.

54. 1 Timothy

55.

56. Titus

57. Philemon

58.

59. James

55.

57. Philemon

58. Hebrews

59.

60. 1 Peter

61. 2 Peter

62.

56.

54. 1 Timothy

55.

56.

57. Philemon

58. Hebrews

59. James

60.

61. 2 Peter

62.

57.

61.

62. 1 John

63. 2 John

64.

58.

58.

59. James

60.

61. 2 Peter

62.

63. 2 John

64.

65. Jude

59.

59.

60. 1 Peter

61. 2 Peter

62. 1 John

63. 2 John

64. 3 John

65.

66. Revelation

60.

56.

57. Philemon

58.

59. James

60. 1 Peter

61.

62. 1 John

63. 2 John

64.

65. Jude

66.

---

4 | Did You Know? (Set 1)

Here is our first set of astonishing facts found by close study of the Holy Scriptures.

- The book of Esther is the only book in the Bible that does not mention the word *God*.
- The Israelites crossed the Red Sea at night, not during the day. The Lord created a "pillar" of a cloud to provide light for the Israelites, while the Egyptians saw only darkness (Exodus 14:19–22).
- There will be no marriages in heaven (Matthew 22:30; Mark 12:25; Luke 20:34–35).

- Luke 19:23 speaks about putting money in the bank to allow it to earn interest.
- Hebrews 13:2 instructs us to always show hospitality to strangers because we may unknowingly be helping an angel.
- Although Joshua wrote the book of Joshua, he could not have written Joshua 24:29–33, which describes his death and Israel after his death.

5 | The Ultimate Books of the Bible Test

Give yourself 5 points for each correct answer.

1. The first book of the Bible is _____.

2. The third book of the Bible is _____.

3. The fifth book of the Bible is _____.

4. The eighth book of the Bible is _____.

5. The ninth book of the Bible is _____.

6. The twelfth book of the Bible is _____.

7. The fifteenth book of the Bible is _____.

8. The eighteenth book of the Bible is _____.

9. The twenty-first book of the Bible is _____.

10. The twenty-second book of the Bible is _____.

11. The twenty-fifth book of the Bible is _____.

12. The twenty-eighth book of the Bible is _____.

13. The thirtieth book of the Bible is _____.

14. The thirty-first book of the Bible is _____.

15. The thirty-third book of the Bible is _____.

16. The thirty-fifth book of the Bible is _____.

17. The thirty-eighth book of the Bible is _____.

18. The last book of the Old Testament is _____.

19. The first book of the New Testament is _____.

20. The third book of the New Testament is _____.

21. The fifth book of the New Testament is _____.

22. The seventh book of the New Testament is _____.

23. The tenth book of the New Testament is _____.

24. The twelfth book of the New Testament is _____.

25. The fourteenth book of the New Testament is
_____.

26. The sixteenth book of the New Testament is
_____.

27. The twentieth book of the New Testament is
_____.

28. The twenty-second book of the New Testament is
_____.

29. The twenty-fifth book of the New Testament is
_____.

30. The last book of the Bible is _____.

6 **Did You Know?** (Set 2)

Here are more interesting facts from the Bible.

- Gabriel, Michael, Lucifer, and Abaddon/Apollyon are the only angels mentioned by name in the Bible (Isaiah 14:12; Luke 1:19; Revelation 9:11, 12:7).

- The apostle Paul was once stoned so thoroughly that his attackers thought he was dead, stopped the stoning, and dragged him out of the city (Acts 14:8–20).
- God ordered Isaiah to walk around stark naked for three years (Isaiah 20:1–4).
- There was a window on Noah's ark (Genesis 6:16).
- The Ten Commandments had writing on both sides of the tablets (Exodus 32:15).
- God caused Aaron's rod to sprout buds that blossomed, producing almonds (Numbers 17:8).
- Jesus, who promises to "come quickly" in the second coming, issues the final promise in the Bible (Revelation 22:20).

7 · 200 Key Verses

Knowing key Scripture passages is essential to becoming a Bible scholar. In this important exercise, you are given 200 verses with one key word missing. If you fill in the missing word correctly, you may reward yourself with 2 points.

1. John 3:16
For God so loved the world, that he gave his only begotten Son, that whosoever _____ in him should not perish, but have everlasting life.

2. John 1:1
In the beginning was the _____, and the Word was with God, and the Word was God.

3. John 14:6
Jesus saith unto him, I am the way, the truth, and the life: no man cometh unto the _____, but by me.

4. Matthew 28:19

Go ye therefore, and teach all _____, baptizing them in the name of the Father, and of the Son, and of the Holy Ghost.

5. Romans 3:23

For all have _____, and come short of the glory of God.

6. Ephesians 2:8

For by _____ are ye saved through faith; and that not of yourselves: it is the gift of God.

7. Genesis 1:1

In the _____ God created the heaven and the earth.

8. Acts 1:8

But ye shall receive _____, after that the Holy Ghost is come upon you: and ye shall be witnesses unto me both in Jerusalem, and in all Judaea, and in Samaria, and unto the uttermost part of the earth.

9. 2 Timothy 3:16

_____ scripture is given by inspiration of God, and is profitable for doctrine, for reproof, for correction, for instruction in righteousness.

10. Romans 10:9

That if thou shalt confess with thy mouth the Lord _____, and shalt believe in thine heart that God hath raised him from the dead, thou shalt be saved.

11. Romans 6:23

For the wages of sin is _____; but the gift of God is eternal life through Jesus Christ our Lord.

12. Acts 2:38

Then Peter said unto them, _____, and be baptized every one of you in the name of Jesus Christ for the remission of sins, and ye shall receive the gift of the Holy Ghost.

13. John 1:12

But as many as received him, to them gave he power to become the sons of God, even to them that _____ on his name.

14. Romans 8:28

And we know that all things work together for _____ to them that love God, to them who are the called according to his purpose.

15. John 1:9

That was the true _____, which lighteth every man that cometh into the world.

16. Genesis 1:26

And God said, Let us make man in our _____, after our likeness: and let them have dominion over the fish of the sea, and over the fowl of the air, and over the cattle, and over all the earth, and over every creeping thing that creepeth upon the earth.

17. Romans 12:1

I beseech you therefore, brethren, by the mercies of God, that ye present your _____ a living sacrifice, holy, acceptable unto God, which is your reasonable service.

18. Romans 5:8

But God commendeth his love toward us, in that, while we were yet _____, Christ died for us.

19. Matthew 28:18

And Jesus came and spake unto them, saying, All _____ is given unto me in heaven and in earth.

20. John 3:3

Jesus answered and said unto him, Verily, verily, I say unto thee, Except a man be _____ again, he cannot see the kingdom of God.

21. Mark 16:15

And he said unto them, Go ye into all the world, and preach the _____ to every creature.

22. John 10:10

The _____ cometh not, but for to steal, and to kill, and to destroy: I am come that they might have life, and that they might have it more abundantly.

23. John 1:14

And the _____ was made flesh, and dwelt among us, (and we beheld his glory, the glory as of the only begotten of the Father,) full of grace and truth.

24. Acts 4:12

Neither is there _____ in any other: for there is none other name under heaven given among men, whereby we must be saved.

25. Acts 2:42

And they continued stedfastly in the apostles' doctrine and fellowship, and in breaking of bread, and in _____.

26. Galatians 5:22

But the fruit of the _____ is love, joy, peace, longsuffering, gentleness, goodness, faith.

27. Proverbs 3:5

_____ in the LORD with all thine heart; and lean not unto thine own understanding.

28. Jeremiah 29:11

For I know the thoughts that I think toward you, saith the LORD, thoughts of peace, and not of _____, to give you an expected end.

29. Titus 3:5

Not by works of righteousness which we have done, but according to his mercy he _____ us, by the washing of regeneration, and renewing of the Holy Ghost.

30. Romans 12:2

And be not conformed to this _____: but be ye transformed by the renewing of your mind, that ye may prove what is that good, and acceptable, and perfect, will of God.

31. John 14:1

Let not your heart be _____: ye believe in God, believe also in me.

32. John 4:1

When therefore the Lord knew how the Pharisees had heard that Jesus made and _____ more disciples than John.

33. Ephesians 4:11

And he gave some, apostles; and some, prophets; and some, _____; and some, pastors and teachers.

34. Romans 5:12

Wherefore, as by one man _____ entered into the world, and death by sin; and so death passed upon all men, for that all have sinned.

35. Matthew 11:28

Come unto me, all ye that labour and are heavy laden, and I will give you _____.

36. Romans 5:1

Therefore being justified by _____, we have peace with God through our Lord Jesus Christ.

37. Genesis 1:27

So God _____ man in his own image, in the image of God created he him; male and female created he them.

38. Romans 1:16

For I am not ashamed of the _____ of Christ: for it is the power of God unto salvation to every one that believeth; to the Jew first, and also to the Greek.

39. 1 John 1:9
If we confess our sins, he is faithful and just to forgive us our sins, and to _____ us from all unrighteousness.

40. Acts 2:1
And when the day of _____ was fully come, they were all with one accord in one place.

41. 2 Corinthians 5:17
Therefore if any man be in _____, he is a new creature: old things are passed away; behold, all things are become new.

42. Hebrews 11:1
Now _____ is the substance of things hoped for, the evidence of things not seen.

43. 2 Timothy 2:15
Study to shew thyself _____ unto God, a workman that needeth not to be ashamed, rightly dividing the word of truth.

44. Romans 8:1
There is therefore now no _____ to them which are in Christ Jesus, who walk not after the flesh, but after the Spirit.

45. Romans 10:13
For whosoever shall call upon the name of the Lord shall be

_____.

46. John 8:32
And ye shall know the truth, and the truth shall make you

_____.

47. Isaiah 9:6
For unto us a child is born, unto us a son is given: and the _____ shall be upon his shoulder: and his name shall be called Wonderful, Counsellor, The mighty God, The everlasting Father, The Prince of Peace.

48. John 14:15

If ye _____ me, keep my commandments.

49. Deuteronomy 6:4

Hear, O Israel: The LORD our God is _____ LORD.

50. John 13:34

A new _____ I give unto you, That ye love one another; as I have loved you, that ye also love one another.

51. John 4:24

God is a Spirit: and they that worship him must worship him in spirit and in _____.

52. Philippians 4:13

I can do all things through _____ which strengtheneth me.

53. Ephesians 2:1

And you hath he quickened, who were dead in trespasses and _____.

54. John 14:16

And I will pray the _____, and he shall give you another Comforter, that he may abide with you for ever.

55. Genesis 1:2

And the earth was without form, and void; and _____ was upon the face of the deep. And the Spirit of God moved upon the face of the waters.

56. Hebrews 4:12

For the word of God is quick, and powerful, and sharper than any twoedged sword, piercing even to the dividing asunder of soul and _____, and of the joints and marrow, and is a discerner of the thoughts and intents of the heart.

57. James 5:16

_____ your faults one to another, and pray one for another, that ye may be healed. The effectual fervent prayer of a righteous man availeth much.

58. Isaiah 7:14

Therefore the Lord himself shall give you a sign; Behold, a _____ shall conceive, and bear a son, and shall call his name Immanuel.

59. John 1:7

The same came for a witness, to bear witness of the Light, that all men through him might _____.

60. John 3:5

Jesus answered, Verily, verily, I say unto thee, Except a man be born of _____ and of the Spirit, he cannot enter into the kingdom of God.

61. Philippians 2:5

Let this _____ be in you, which was also in Christ Jesus.

62. John 1:29

The next day John seeth Jesus coming unto him, and saith, Behold the Lamb of God, which taketh away the _____ of the world.

63. Romans 1:18

For the _____ of God is revealed from heaven against all ungodliness and unrighteousness of men, who hold the truth in unrighteousness.

64. Philippians 4:6

Be careful for _____; but in every thing by prayer and supplication with thanksgiving let your requests be made known unto God.

65. Hebrews 12:1

Wherefore seeing we also are compassed about with so great a cloud of _____, let us lay aside every weight, and the sin which doth so easily beset us, and let us run with patience the race that is set before us.

66. John 1:3

    All things were _____ by him; and without him was not any thing made that was made.

67. Matthew 16:18

    And I say also unto thee, That thou art Peter, and upon this _____ I will build my church; and the gates of hell shall not prevail against it.

68. Galatians 2:20

    I am _____ with Christ: nevertheless I live; yet not I, but Christ liveth in me: and the life which I now live in the flesh I live by the faith of the Son of God, who loved me, and gave himself for me.

69. Matthew 25:31

    When the Son of man shall come in his glory, and all the holy angels with him, then shall he sit upon the _____ of his glory.

70. Matthew 5:17

    Think not that I am come to destroy the law, or the prophets: I am not come to destroy, but to _____.

71. Romans 10:17

    So then _____ cometh by hearing, and hearing by the word of God.

72. Matthew 6:33

    But seek ye first the kingdom of God, and his _____; and all these things shall be added unto you.

73. Luke 4:18

    The _____ of the Lord is upon me, because he hath anointed me to preach the gospel to the poor; he hath sent me to heal the brokenhearted, to preach deliverance to the captives, and recovering of sight to the blind, to set at liberty them that are bruised.

74. John 16:13

Howbeit when he, the Spirit of _____, is come, he
will guide you into all truth: for he shall not speak of himself;
but whatsoever he shall hear, that shall he speak: and he will
shew you things to come.

75. Acts 20:28

Take heed therefore unto yourselves, and to all the flock,
over the which the Holy Ghost hath made you overseers, to
feed the church of God, which he hath purchased with his
own _____.

76. Titus 2:11

For the grace of God that bringeth _____ hath ap-
peared to all men.

77. John 8:44

Ye are of your father the devil, and the lusts of your father
ye will do. He was a murderer from the beginning, and
abode not in the _____, because there is no truth
in him. When he speaketh a lie, he speaketh of his own: for
he is a liar, and the father of it.

78. Ephesians 6:10

Finally, my brethren, be strong in the Lord, and in the
_____ of his might.

79. Romans 13:1

Let every soul be subject unto the higher powers. For there
is no power but of _____: the powers that be are
ordained of God.

80. John 2:15

And when he had made a scourge of small cords, he drove
them all out of the temple, and the sheep, and the oxen;
and poured out the changers' money, and overthrew the
_____.

81. Mark 16:16

He that believeth and is _____ shall be saved; but he that believeth not shall be damned.

82. Romans 3:10

As it is written, There is none _____, no, not one.

83. Genesis 3:15

And I will put enmity between thee and the _____, and between thy seed and her seed; it shall bruise thy head, and thou shalt bruise his heel.

84. Hebrews 11:6

But without _____ it is impossible to please him: for he that cometh to God must believe that he is, and that he is a rewarder of them that diligently seek him.

85. John 14:26

But the Comforter, which is the Holy Ghost, whom the _____ will send in my name, he shall teach you all things, and bring all things to your remembrance, whatsoever I have said unto you.

86. John 5:24

Verily, verily, I say unto you, He that heareth my word, and believeth on him that sent me, hath everlasting life, and shall not come into condemnation; but is passed from _____ unto life.

87. Joel 2:28

And it shall come to pass afterward, that I will pour out my _____ upon all flesh; and your sons and your daughters shall prophesy, your old men shall dream dreams, your young men shall see visions.

88. Genesis 1:11

And God said, Let the earth bring forth grass, the herb yielding seed, and the fruit tree yielding fruit after his _____, whose seed is in itself, upon the earth: and it was so.

89. James 1:2
My brethren, count it all _____ when ye fall into divers temptations.

90. Colossians 1:15
Who is the image of the invisible God, the _____ of every creature.

91. Matthew 22:37
Jesus said unto him, Thou shalt love the Lord thy God with all thy heart, and with all thy soul, and with all thy _____.

92. Titus 2:13
Looking for that blessed _____, and the glorious appearing of the great God and our Saviour Jesus Christ.

93. Philippians 4:8
Finally, brethren, whatsoever things are true, whatsoever things are honest, whatsoever things are just, whatso-ever things are pure, whatsoever things are lovely, whatso-ever things are of good report; if there be any virtue, and if there be any _____, think on these things.

94. Acts 1:9
And when he had spoken these things, while they beheld, he was taken up; and a _____ received him out of their sight.

95. John 4:7
There cometh a woman of _____ to draw water: Jesus saith unto her, Give me to drink.

96. Micah 6:8
He hath shewed thee, O man, what is good; and what doth the LORD require of thee, but to do justly, and to love mercy, and to walk _____ with thy God?

97. John 17:17
_____ them through thy truth: thy word is truth.

98. Acts 20:7

And upon the first day of the week, when the disciples came together to break bread, _____ preached unto them, ready to depart on the morrow; and continued his speech until midnight.

99. Acts 16:31

And they said, Believe on the Lord Jesus Christ, and thou shalt be saved, and thy _____.

100. John 11:25

Jesus said unto her, I am the _____, and the life: he that believeth in me, though he were dead, yet shall he live.

101. John 8:58

Jesus said unto them, Verily, verily, I say unto you, Before _____ was, I am.

102. Acts 2:4

And they were all filled with the Holy Ghost, and began to speak with other _____, as the Spirit gave them utterance.

103. John 15:5

I am the vine, ye are the _____: He that abideth in me, and I in him, the same bringeth forth much fruit: for without me ye can do nothing.

104. Acts 2:41

Then they that gladly received his word were _____: and the same day there were added unto them about three thousand souls.

105. Proverbs 22:6

Train up a _____ in the way he should go: and when he is old, he will not depart from it.

106. Genesis 3:1

Now the _____ was more subtil than any beast of the field which the LORD God had made. And he said unto the woman, Yea, hath God said, Ye shall not eat of every tree of the garden?

107. James 1:5

If any of you lack _____, let him ask of God, that giveth to all men liberally, and upbraideth not; and it shall be given him.

108. Hebrews 1:1

God, who at sundry times and in divers manners spake in time past unto the fathers by the _____.

109. 2 John 1:2

For the _____ sake, which dwelleth in us, and shall be with us for ever.

110. John 17:3

And this is life _____, that they might know thee the only true God, and Jesus Christ, whom thou hast sent.

111. John 5:7

The impotent man answered him, Sir, I have no man, when the _____ is troubled, to put me into the pool: but while I am coming, another steppeth down before me.

112. John 8:31

Then said Jesus to those Jews which believed on him, If ye continue in my word, then are ye my _____ indeed.

113. Luke 1:4

That thou mightest know the certainty of those things, wherein thou hast been _____.

114. Revelation 3:20

Behold, I stand at the door, and knock: if any man hear my _____, and open the door, I will come in to him, and will sup with him, and he with me.

115. 1 Peter 2:3

If so be ye have _____ that the Lord is gracious.

116. John 10:30

I and my _____ are one.

117. 1 Peter 3:15

But sanctify the Lord God in your hearts: and be ready always to give an answer to every man that asketh you a reason of the _____ that is in you with meekness and fear.

118. Matthew 7:21

Not every one that saith unto me, Lord, Lord, shall enter into the kingdom of heaven; but he that doeth the _____ of my Father which is in heaven.

119. John 3:18

He that believeth on him is not condemned: but he that believeth not is condemned already, because he hath not believed in the name of the only _____ Son of God.

120. Genesis 12:1

Now the Lᴏʀᴅ had said unto _____, Get thee out of thy country, and from thy kindred, and from thy father's house, unto a land that I will shew thee.

121. John 3:8

The wind bloweth where it listeth, and thou hearest the sound thereof, but canst not tell whence it cometh, and whither it goeth: so is every one that is born of the

_____.

122. John 15:1

I am the true _____, and my Father is the husbandman.

123. Genesis 2:7

And the Lᴏʀᴅ God formed man of the dust of the ground, and breathed into his nostrils the breath of _____; and man became a living soul.

124. Genesis 1:3

And God said, _____ there be light: and there was light.

125. John 8:12

Then spake Jesus again unto them, saying, I am the
_____ of the world: he that followeth me shall not
walk in darkness, but shall have the light of life.

126. 1 Peter 2:9

But ye are a _____ generation, a royal priesthood,
an holy nation, a peculiar people; that ye should shew forth
the praises of him who hath called you out of darkness into
his marvellous light.

127. Luke 1:26

And in the _____ month the angel Gabriel was sent
from God unto a city of Galilee, named Nazareth.

128. Hebrews 9:27

And as it is appointed unto men once to die, but after this
the _____.

129. John 3:2

The same came to Jesus by night, and said unto him,
_____, we know that thou art a teacher come from
God: for no man can do these miracles that thou doest, except God be with him.

130. Matthew 5:14

Ye are the _____ of the world. A city that is set on
an hill cannot be hid.

131. Exodus 3:14

And God said unto _____, I Am That I Am: and he
said, Thus shalt thou say unto the children of Israel, I Am
hath sent me unto you.

132. 1 Corinthians 6:9

Know ye not that the unrighteous shall not inherit the kingdom of God? Be not _____: neither fornicators,
nor idolaters, nor adulterers, nor effeminate, nor abusers of
themselves with mankind.

133. Luke 10:25

And, behold, a certain lawyer stood up, and tempted him, saying, Master, what shall I do to inherit eternal _____?

134. Matthew 7:7

_____, and it shall be given you; seek, and ye shall find; knock, and it shall be opened unto you.

135. Ephesians 1:3

_____ be the God and Father of our Lord Jesus Christ, who hath blessed us with all spiritual blessings in heavenly places in Christ.

136. Matthew 1:18

Now the _____ of Jesus Christ was on this wise: When as his mother Mary was espoused to Joseph, before they came together, she was found with child of the Holy Ghost.

137. Romans 1:20

For the invisible things of him from the creation of the world are clearly seen, being understood by the things that are made, even his eternal power and Godhead; so that they are without _____.

138. John 8:9

And they which heard it, being convicted by their own conscience, went out one by one, beginning at the eldest, even unto the last: and _____ was left alone, and the woman standing in the midst.

139. John 1:5

And the _____ shineth in darkness; and the darkness comprehended it not.

140. 1 Thessalonians 4:13

But I would not have you to be ignorant, brethren, concerning them which are asleep, that ye sorrow not, even as others which have no _____.

141. Hebrews 13:5

Let your conversation be without covetousness; and be content with such things as ye have: for he hath said, I will never leave thee, nor _____ thee.

142. 1 John 4:1

Beloved, believe not every _____, but try the spirits whether they are of God: because many false prophets are gone out into the world.

143. James 1:17

Every good _____ and every perfect gift is from above, and cometh down from the Father of lights, with whom is no variableness, neither shadow of turning.

144. Matthew 6:19

Lay not up for yourselves _____ upon earth, where moth and rust doth corrupt, and where thieves break through and steal.

145. Isaiah 61:1

The Spirit of the Lord God is upon me; because the Lord hath anointed me to _____ good tidings unto the meek; he hath sent me to bind up the brokenhearted, to proclaim liberty to the captives, and the opening of the prison to them that are bound.

146. Galatians 3:28

There is neither Jew nor Greek, there is neither bond nor free, there is neither male nor female: for ye are all _____ in Christ Jesus.

147. 2 Peter 3:9

The Lord is not slack concerning his _____, as some men count slackness; but is longsuffering to us-ward, not willing that any should perish, but that all should come to repentance.

148. Acts 1:11

Which also said, Ye men of Galilee, why stand ye gazing up into heaven? this same _____, which is taken up from you into heaven, shall so come in like manner as ye have seen him go into heaven.

149. James 5:14

Is any _____ among you? let him call for the elders of the church; and let them pray over him, anointing him with oil in the name of the Lord.

150. John 3:36

He that believeth on the _____ hath everlasting life: and he that believeth not the Son shall not see life; but the wrath of God abideth on him.

151. Ephesians 6:12

For we wrestle not against flesh and blood, but against _____, against powers, against the rulers of the darkness of this world, against spiritual wickedness in high places.

152. Matthew 6:9

After this manner therefore _____ ye: Our Father which art in heaven, Hallowed be thy name.

153. Acts 3:19

_____ ye therefore, and be converted, that your sins may be blotted out, when the times of refreshing shall come from the presence of the Lord.

154. James 2:14

What doth it profit, my brethren, though a man say he hath faith, and have not works? can _____ save him?

155. Isaiah 40:31

But they that wait upon the _____ shall renew their strength; they shall mount up with wings as eagles; they shall run, and not be weary; and they shall walk, and not faint.

156. John 3:17

For God sent not his Son into the world to condemn
the world; but that the world through him might be
_____.

157. Luke 1:35

And the _____ answered and said unto her, The
Holy Ghost shall come upon thee, and the power of the
Highest shall overshadow thee: therefore also that holy thing
which shall be born of thee shall be called the Son of God.

158. Genesis 1:28

And God blessed them, and God said unto them, Be
_____, and multiply, and replenish the earth, and
subdue it: and have dominion over the fish of the sea, and
over the fowl of the air, and over every living thing that
moveth upon the earth.

159. Ephesians 2:10

For we are his _____, created in Christ Jesus unto
good works, which God hath before ordained that we should
walk in them.

160. 2 Corinthians 5:21

For he hath made him to be _____ for us, who
knew no sin; that we might be made the righteousness of
God in him.

161. Romans 6:1

What shall we say then? Shall we continue in sin, that
_____ may abound?

162. Ephesians 1:13

In whom ye also trusted, after that ye heard the word of
truth, the gospel of your _____: in whom also
after that ye believed, ye were sealed with that holy Spirit of
promise.

163. Romans 6:3

Know ye not, that so many of us as were baptized into Jesus
Christ were baptized into his _____?

164. Matthew 18:15

Moreover if thy _____ shall trespass against thee, go and tell him his fault between thee and him alone: if he shall hear thee, thou hast gained thy brother.

165. 1 John 4:5

They are of the _____: therefore speak they of the world, and the world heareth them.

166. James 1:27

Pure religion and undefiled before God and the Father is this, To visit the fatherless and _____ in their afflic-tion, and to keep himself unspotted from the world.

167. John 16:33

These things I have spoken unto you, that in me ye might have peace. In the world ye shall have tribulation: but be of good cheer; I have _____ the world.

168. John 5:28

Marvel not at this: for the hour is coming, in the which all that are in the _____ shall hear his voice.

169. John 5:39

Search the _____; for in them ye think ye have eternal life: and they are they which testify of me.

170. Titus 2:3

The aged _____ likewise, that they be in behaviour as becometh holiness, not false accusers, not given to much wine, teachers of good things.

171. John 4:23

But the hour cometh, and now is, when the true _____ shall worship the Father in spirit and in truth: for the Father seeketh such to worship him.

172. Matthew 7:1

_____ not, that ye be not judged.

173. 1 Timothy 2:5

For there is one God, and one _____ between God and men, the man Christ Jesus.

174. Matthew 4:1

Then was Jesus led up of the Spirit into the _____
to be tempted of the devil.

175. John 1:18

No man hath seen _____ at any time, the only
begotten Son, which is in the bosom of the Father, he hath
declared him.

176. Ephesians 4:1

I therefore, the _____ of the Lord, beseech you
that ye walk worthy of the vocation wherewith ye are called.

177. Ephesians 5:18

And be not drunk with wine, wherein is excess; but be filled
with the _____.

178. Ephesians 5:22

Wives, _____ yourselves unto your own husbands,
as unto the Lord.

179. Revelation 21:1

And I saw a new heaven and a new earth: for the first heaven
and the first earth were passed away; and there was no
more _____.

180. 2 Peter 3:4

And saying, Where is the promise of his _____? for
since the fathers fell asleep, all things continue as they were
from the beginning of the creation.

181. John 6:44

No man can come to me, except the _____ which
hath sent me draw him: and I will raise him up at the last day.

182. John 20:19

Then the same day at evening, being the first day of the
week, when the doors were shut where the _____
were assembled for fear of the Jews, came Jesus and stood
in the midst, and saith unto them, Peace be unto you.

183. Psalm 119:105

Thy word is a _____ unto my feet, and a light unto my path.

184. Genesis 2:18

And the LORD God said, It is not good that the _____ should be alone; I will make him an help meet for him.

185. 1 John 1:7

But if we walk in the light, as he is in the light, we have _____ one with another, and the blood of Jesus Christ his Son cleanseth us from all sin.

186. 1 Corinthians 15:3

For I delivered unto you first of all that which I also received, how that Christ died for our _____ according to the scriptures.

187. Isaiah 53:5

But he was _____ for our transgressions, he was bruised for our iniquities: the chastisement of our peace was upon him; and with his stripes we are healed.

188. Ephesians 1:7

In whom we have _____ through his blood, the forgiveness of sins, according to the riches of his grace.

189. Ephesians 5:25

Husbands, love your wives, even as Christ also loved the _____, and gave himself for it.

190. Romans 8:9

But ye are not in the _____, but in the Spirit, if so be that the Spirit of God dwell in you. Now if any man have not the Spirit of Christ, he is none of his.

191. John 15:13

Greater _____ hath no man than this, that a man lay down his life for his friends.

192. Galatians 5:16

This I say then, Walk in the _____, and ye shall not fulfil the lust of the flesh.

193. John 3:14

And as _____ lifted up the serpent in the wilderness, even so must the Son of man be lifted up.

194. John 3:4

Nicodemus saith unto him, How can a man be _____ when he is old? can he enter the second time into his mother's womb, and be born?

195. Matthew 7:13

Enter ye in at the strait _____: for wide is the gate, and broad is the way, that leadeth to destruction, and many there be which go in thereat.

196. James 1:22

But be ye doers of the word, and not hearers only, _____ your own selves.

197. Genesis 2:24

Therefore shall a man leave his father and his mother, and shall cleave unto his _____: and they shall be one flesh.

198. John 10:27

My _____ hear my voice, and I know them, and they follow me.

199. Colossians 1:16

For by him were all things _____, that are in heaven, and that are in earth, visible and invisible, whether they be thrones, or dominions, or principalities, or powers: all things were created by him, and for him.

200. Colossians 3:1

If ye then be risen with _____, seek those things which are above, where Christ sitteth on the right hand of God.

8 Did You Know? (Set 3)

Here are more facts that amaze.

- The youngest book of the Old Testament is the book of Malachi, written approximately 400 BC.
- Delilah did not cut Samson's hair. She called someone else to do it (Judges 16:19).
- There is a city named Sin in the book of Ezekiel (30:15).
- Although ivory is mentioned thirteen times in the Bible, elephants, the source of the ivory, are not mentioned at all.
- The longest single sentence in the King James Bible features the genealogy of Jesus and spans sixteen verses from Luke 3:23 all the way through Luke 3:38.
- There are at least five women named Mary in the New Testament.
- An unidentified son of a prophet once told a man to strike him. The man refused to strike the prophet's son and was told that because he refused, he would be killed by a lion. He was indeed killed in a lion attack (1 Kings 20:35–36).

9 The Ten Plagues Inflicted on Egypt

To be Bible brilliant and not just Bible literate, you must have a thorough understanding of the ten plagues God inflicted on Egypt in Exodus 7:14–12:30. God sent the plagues as a warning that there is only one true God. The Egyptians worshiped a multitude of false gods, and the Lord used the plagues to prove that nothing worshiped in Egypt could save them from his demonstrative power.

This tutorial will explain the ten plagues and their order. This section concludes with seven fill-in-the-blank questions to test your knowledge of the ten plagues.

Plague 1: Water Turned into Blood

God turned water throughout Egypt into blood. Fish and river animals died, and the Nile River reeked. The account of the first plague is in Exodus 7:14–25.

Plague 2: Frogs

The Lord saturated the land of Egypt with an abundance of frogs. Later, in yet another display of his power, God supernaturally killed the frogs, filling Egypt with the stench of their death. The full account of the second plague is in Exodus 8:1–15.

Plague 3: Lice

God sent an infestation of the wingless, biting parasites known as lice. The infestation was so thick that, according to Exodus 8:17, "All the dust of the land became lice throughout all the land of Egypt." The full account is in Exodus 8:16–19.

Plague 4: Flies

God sent massive, intrusive swarms of flies upon Egypt. Flies covered the ground, harassed the people, and invaded all the Egyptian homes. To prove he was God alone and that this plague was only for Egyptians, no flies invaded Goshen, where God's people, the Israelites, lived. This account is in Exodus 8:20–32.

Plague 5: Death of Livestock

God killed Egypt's cattle, horses, donkeys, camels, oxen, and sheep during the fifth plague. No livestock of the Israelites died during this time. This plague is detailed in Exodus 9:1–7.

Plague 6: Boils

God sent the sixth plague to Egypt without any warning. The sixth plague resulted in festering boils and an incurable itch on all the Egyptians. The boils were so bad that Pharaoh's magicians could not stand before Moses. The account of this plague is in Exodus 9:8–12.

Plague 7: Hailstorm

God provided prior warning before unleashing the worst hailstorm in Egypt's existence. The entire account is in Exodus 9:13–34.

Plague 8: Locusts

God sent swarms of locusts into Egypt that were so dense the land became dark because of them. Yet no locusts intruded into Goshen, where the Israelites were safe from the infestation. The account is in Exodus 10:1–20.

Plague 9: Darkness

Darkness "which may be felt" covered Egypt for three days. The darkness was so intense that, according to Exodus 10:21–23, people could not see each other. The Israelites, however, enjoyed light as usual.

Plague 10: Death of All Firstborn

The firstborn of the Egyptian people and the firstborn of their beasts were slain in the tenth and final plague. All deaths occurred in a single night. To show a clear distinction between the Egyptians and God's beloved Israelites, the Lord said the Israelites' peace on that historically gruesome night would be so complete that not even an Israelite dog would bark at a person or animal. The account is in Exodus 11:1–8; 12:21–30.

In the following exercise, take your time and try to fill in the missing plagues in the lists. In each case, the list is in order. This will help you to learn not only the plagues but also the order in which they occurred. Give yourself 10 points for each of the twenty-eight blanks you fill in correctly.

1.

    1.

    2. Frogs

    3. Lice

2.

    4. Flies

    5.

    6. Boils

3.

    7. Hailstorm

    8. Locusts

    9.

    10. Death of all firstborn

4.

    1.

    2. Frogs

    3. Lice

    4.

    5.

6. Boils
7. Hailstorm
8.
9.
10. Death of all firstborn

5.

1. Water turned into blood
2.
3.
4. Flies
5. Death of livestock
6.
7.
8. Locusts
9. Darkness
10. Death of all firstborn

6.

1. Water turned into blood
2.
3.
4.
5. Death of livestock
6.
7.
8. Locusts
9.
10. Death of all firstborn

You knew this was coming. Try to fill in each plague in the order in which it occurred.

7.

1.

2.

3.

4.

5.

6.

7.

8.

9.

10.

All about Money

In the following exercises that teach God's wisdom in money affairs, take the words under each Scripture passage and put them in the appropriate blanks. By studying which word goes into which blank, you will learn what God desires us to know about money. Give yourself 2 points for each passage you complete accurately.

Any repeats of passages throughout the various money topics are intentional.

10 Debt

1. Exodus 22:14
And if a man _____ ought of his neighbour, and it be _____, or _____, the owner thereof being not with it, he shall surely make it _____.

> hurt   die   good   borrow

2. Deuteronomy 15:6
For the LORD thy God blesseth thee, as he _____ thee: and thou shalt lend unto many _____, but thou shalt not _____; and thou shalt _____ over many nations, but they shall not reign over thee.

> reign   nations   promised   borrow

3. Deuteronomy 28:12
The LORD shall open unto thee his good _____, the _____ to give the rain unto thy land in his _____, and to bless all the work of thine _____: and thou shalt lend unto many _____, and thou shalt not borrow.

> season   heaven   nations   hand   treasure

4. 2 Kings 4:7
Then she came and told the man of _____. And he said, Go, sell the _____, and pay thy _____, and live thou and thy _____ of the rest.

> debt   children   oil   God

5. Psalm 37:21

The wicked borroweth, and _____ not again: but
the _____ sheweth _____, and giveth.

> payeth   righteous   mercy

6. Proverbs 22:7

The _____ ruleth over the _____, and
the _____ is servant to the _____.

> poor   lender   borrower   rich

7. Proverbs 22:26–27

Be not thou one of them that strike _____, or of
them that are _____ for _____. If thou
hast _____ to pay, why should he take away thy
_____ from under thee?

> sureties   bed   nothing   hands   debts

8. Ecclesiastes 5:5

_____ is it that thou shouldest not
_____, than that thou shouldest vow and not
_____.

> pay   vow   better

9. Romans 13:8

Owe no _____ any thing, but to love one
_____: for he that loveth another hath fulfilled the
_____.

> law   another   man

11 Wealth

1. Exodus 23:12

Six days thou shalt do thy work, and on the _____ day thou shalt rest: that thine _____ and thine ass may rest, and the son of thy _____, and the _____, may be _____.

> refreshed   handmaid   ox   stranger   seventh

2. Proverbs 12:11

He that tilleth his _____ shall be satisfied with _____: but he that followeth _____ persons is _____ of understanding.

> vain   void   land   bread

3. Proverbs 13:11

_____ gotten by _____ shall be _____: but he that gathereth by labour shall _____.

> increase   vanity   diminished   wealth

4. Proverbs 14:15

The _____ believeth every _____: but the prudent _____ looketh _____ to his going.

> man   simple   word   well

5. Proverbs 19:2

Also, that the soul be without _____, it is not _____; and he that hasteth with his

_____ _____.

| feet   sinneth   knowledge   good |

6. Proverbs 21:5

The _____ of the _____ _____ only to plenteousness; but of _____ one that is _____ only to want.

| diligent   hasty   thoughts   tend   every |

7. Proverbs 23:4

_____ not to be _____: cease from _____ own _____.

| rich   wisdom   thine   labour |

8. Proverbs 28:19–20

He that tilleth his land shall have plenty of _____: but he that followeth after _____ persons shall have _____ enough. A faithful man shall abound with blessings: but he that maketh haste to be _____ shall not be _____.

| innocent   poverty   vain   bread   rich |

12 Being Happy with What You Have

1. Psalm 23:1

The _____ is my _____; I shall not _____.

> shepherd   want   LORD

2. Ecclesiastes 5:10

He that loveth _____ shall not be satisfied with silver; nor he that loveth _____ with _____: this is also _____.

> vanity   silver   increase   abundance

3. Matthew 6:31–33

Therefore take no _____, saying, What shall we eat? or, What shall we _____? or, Wherewithal shall we be _____? (For after all these things do the _____ seek:) for your heavenly Father knoweth that ye have need of all these things. But seek ye first the kingdom of God, and his _____; and all these things shall be added unto you.

> clothed   Gentiles   righteousness   drink   thought

4. Luke 3:14

And the _____ likewise demanded of him, saying, And what shall we do? And he said unto them, Do _____ to no man, neither accuse any _____; and be content with your _____.

> wages   falsely   violence   soldiers

5. Philippians 4:11–13

   Not that I speak in respect of want: for I have learned,
   in whatsoever _____ I am, therewith to be
   _____. I know both how to be abased, and I
   know how to abound: every where and in all things I am
   _____ both to be full and to be _____,
   both to abound and to suffer need. I can do all things
   through _____ which strengtheneth me.

   > content   hungry   state   instructed   Christ

6. 1 Thessalonians 4:11

   And that ye study to be _____, and to do your own
   _____, and to work with your own _____,
   as we _____ you.

   > quiet   business   commanded   hands

7. 1 Timothy 6:6

   But _____ with _____ is great
   _____.

   > gain   godliness   contentment

8. 1 Timothy 6:7–10

   For we brought nothing into this world, and it is certain we
   can carry nothing out. And having food and _____
   let us be therewith content. But they that will be rich fall
   into temptation and a snare, and into many _____
   and hurtful _____, which drown men in
   _____ and perdition. For the love of money is the
   root of all evil: which while some coveted after, they have
   erred from the _____, and pierced themselves
   through with many _____.

   > faith   raiment   lusts   foolish   destruction   sorrows

9. Hebrews 13:5

Let your _____ be without covetousness; and be content with such things as ye have: for he hath said, I will _____ leave thee, nor _____ thee.

> forsake   conversation   never

10. James 4:1–3

From whence come _____ and fightings among you? come they not hence, even of your lusts that _____ in your _____? Ye lust, and have not: ye kill, and desire to have, and cannot obtain: ye fight and war, yet ye have not, because ye ask not. Ye _____, and receive not, because ye ask amiss, that ye may _____ it upon your lusts.

> consume   ask   members   wars   war

13 Giving and Being Generous

1. Deuteronomy 15:10

Thou shalt surely give him, and thine _____ shall not be grieved when thou givest unto him: because that for this thing the _____ thy God shall _____ thee in all thy _____, and in all that thou puttest thine _____ unto.

> hand   bless   works   heart   Lord

2. Deuteronomy 16:17

Every _____ shall give as he is able, according to the _____ of the LORD thy _____ which he hath given _____.

> thee   man   God   blessing

3. 1 Chronicles 29:9

Then the _____ rejoiced, for that they offered willingly, because with perfect _____ they offered willingly to the _____: and _____ the _____ also rejoiced with great joy.

> LORD   David   people   heart   king

4. Proverbs 3:9–10

Honour the LORD with thy _____, and with the _____ of all thine increase: So shall thy _____ be filled with plenty, and thy _____ shall burst out with new _____.

> presses   firstfruits   wine   substance   barns

5. Proverbs 3:27

Withhold not _____ from them to whom it is _____, when it is in the _____ of thine _____ to do it.

> hand   power   good   due

6. Proverbs 11:24–25

There is that _____, and yet _____;
and there is that withholdeth more than is meet, but
it tendeth to poverty. The liberal _____ shall
be made _____: and he that watereth shall be
_____ also himself.

> increaseth   fat   scattereth · soul   watered

7. Proverbs 21:26

He _____ _____ all the _____
long: but the righteous giveth and _____ not.

> day   coveteth   spareth   greedily

8. Proverbs 22:9

He that hath a bountiful _____ shall be
_____; for he giveth of his _____ to the
_____.

> bread   poor   eye   blessed

9. Proverbs 28:27

He that giveth unto the _____ shall not
_____: but he that hideth his _____ shall
have many a _____.

> lack   eyes   curse   poor

10. Malachi 3:10

Bring ye all the tithes into the _____, that there may be meat in mine house, and prove me now herewith, saith the _____ of _____, if I will not open you the windows of heaven, and pour you out a _____, that there shall not be _____ enough to receive it.

> blessing   storehouse   hosts   room   LORD

11. Matthew 6:3–4

But when thou doest _____, let not thy left _____ know what thy right hand doeth: That thine alms may be in _____: and thy _____ which seeth in secret himself shall reward _____ openly.

> secret   alms   Father   thee   hand

12. Mark 12:41–44

And Jesus sat over against the _____, and beheld how the people _____ money into the treasury: and many that were rich cast in much. And there came a certain poor widow, and she threw in two mites, which make a farthing. And he called unto him his disciples, and saith unto them, Verily I say unto you, That this poor widow hath cast more in, than all they which have cast into the treasury: For all they did cast in of their _____; but she of her want did cast in all that she had, even all her _____.

> cast   living   treasury   abundance

13. Luke 3:11

He _____ and saith unto them, He that hath two _____, let him _____ to him that hath _____; and he that hath _____, let him do likewise.

> meat   coats   impart   answereth   none

14. Luke 6:30

Give to every _____ that asketh of _____; and of him that taketh away thy _____ ask them not again.

> thee   man   goods

15. Luke 6:38

Give, and it shall be given unto you; good measure, pressed down, and _____ together, and _____ over, shall men give into your _____. For with the same measure that ye mete withal it shall be _____ to you again.

> measured   shaken   running   bosom

16. Acts 20:35

I have shewed you all _____, how that so _____ ye ought to support the weak, and to remember the words of the Lord _____, how he said, It is more _____ to give than to receive.

> labouring   blessed   Jesus   things

17. Romans 12:8

Or he that exhorteth, on _____: he that
giveth, let him do it with _____; he that ruleth, with _____; he that sheweth mercy, with
_____.

diligence   cheerfulness   exhortation   simplicity

18. 2 Corinthians 9:6–8

But this I say, He which _____ sparingly shall reap
also sparingly; and he which soweth bountifully shall reap
also bountifully. Every man according as he purposeth in his
_____, so let him give; not _____, or of
necessity: for God loveth a cheerful giver. And God is able to
make all grace _____ toward you; that ye, always
having all _____ in all things, may abound to every
good _____.

grudgingly   heart   soweth   abound   work   sufficiency

19. 2 Corinthians 9:10

Now he that ministereth _____ to the sower both
minister _____ for your _____, and multiply your seed sown, and increase the _____ of
your righteousness.

fruits   seed   food   bread

20. Galatians 6:7

Be not deceived; _____ is not _____:
for whatsoever a man _____, that shall he also
_____.

reap   God   mocked   soweth

21. Philippians 4:15–17

Now ye Philippians know also, that in the beginning of the _____, when I departed from Macedonia, no _____ communicated with me as concerning giving and receiving, but ye only. For even in Thessalonica ye sent once and again unto my _____. Not because I desire a gift: but I desire _____ that may _____ to your _____.

| account church necessity abound fruit gospel |

22. James 2:15–16

If a brother or _____ be naked, and destitute of daily _____, And one of you say unto them, Depart in peace, be ye warmed and _____; notwithstanding ye give them not those things which are needful to the _____; what doth it _____?

| filled body sister food profit |

14 Receiving

Note that there are far more passages on giving than on receiving.

1. Ecclesiastes 5:19

Every man also to whom _____ hath given riches and wealth, and hath given him power to eat thereof, and to take his _____, and to rejoice in his _____; this is the _____ of God.

| labour God gift portion |

2. John 3:27

_____ answered and said, A _____
can receive _____, except it be given him from
_____.

> man   John   heaven   nothing

3. Acts 20:35

I have shewed you all things, how that so _____ ye
ought to support the _____, and to remember the
_____ of the Lord Jesus, how he said, It is more
_____ to give than to receive.

> words   blessed   labouring   weak

4. 1 Corinthians 9:10–11

Or saith he it altogether for our sakes? For our sakes, no
doubt, this is _____: that he that _____
should plow in hope; and that he that _____ in
hope should be partaker of his hope. If we have sown unto
you spiritual _____, is it a great thing if we shall
reap your _____ things?

> written   thresheth   things   ploweth   carnal

5. 1 Timothy 5:18

For the _____ saith, thou shalt not _____
the _____ that treadeth out the corn. And, The
_____ is worthy of his _____.

> labourer   reward   muzzle   scripture   ox

15 Running a Business

1. Leviticus 19:13

_____ shalt not defraud thy _____, neither rob him: the _____ of him that is hired shall not abide with _____ all night until the _____.

> neighbour   thou   wages   morning   thee

2. Deuteronomy 25:13–15

Thou shalt not have in thy _____ divers weights, a great and a small. Thou shalt not have in thine house divers measures, a great and a small. But thou shalt have a _____ and just _____, a perfect and just _____ shalt thou have: that thy days may be lengthened in the land which the LORD thy _____ giveth thee.

> measure   bag   weight   God   perfect

3. Job 31:13–14

If I did despise the cause of my _____ or of my maidservant, when they contended with me; What then shall I do when God _____ up? and when he _____, what shall I answer him?

> riseth   visiteth   manservant

4. Psalm 112:5

A good man sheweth _____, and _____: he will guide his _____ with _____.

> affairs   favour   discretion   lendeth

5. Proverbs 10:4

He becometh _____ that _____ with a slack _____: but the hand of the _____ maketh rich.

dealeth   diligent   poor   hand

6. Proverbs 11:1

A false _____ is _____ to the _____: but a just weight is his _____.

delight   abomination   LORD   balance

7. Proverbs 13:4

The _____ of the _____ desireth, and hath _____: but the soul of the diligent shall be made _____.

sluggard   soul   fat   nothing

8. Proverbs 13:11

_____ gotten by _____ shall be diminished: but he that gathereth by _____ shall _____.

labour   vanity   wealth   increase

9. Proverbs 16:8

_____ is a little with _____ than great _____ without _____.

revenues   right   righteousness   better

10. Proverbs 22:16

He that _____ the _____ to increase his
_____, and he that giveth to the _____,
shall surely come to want.

> riches oppresseth rich poor

11. Jeremiah 22:13

Woe unto him that _____ his house by unrighteousness, and his chambers by wrong; that useth his neighbour's _____ without _____, and giveth
him not for his _____.

> wages work buildeth service

12. Malachi 3:5

And I will come near to you to judgment; and I will be
a swift witness against the sorcerers, and against the
_____, and against false _____, and
against those that oppress the _____ in his wages,
the widow, and the fatherless, and that turn aside the
stranger from his right, and _____ not me, saith
the LORD of _____.

> hosts fear adulterers hireling swearers

13. Luke 16:10

He that is faithful in that which is _____ is
_____ also in much: and he that is _____
in the least is unjust also in _____.

> faithful unjust much least

14. Ephesians 6:9

And, ye masters, do the same _____ unto them, forbearing threatening: knowing that your _____ also is in _____; neither is there respect of _____ with him.

heaven   Master   persons   things

15. Colossians 4:1

_____, give unto your _____ that which is just and equal; knowing that ye also have a _____ in _____.

servants   heaven   Master   masters

16. James 5:4

Behold, the hire of the _____ who have reaped down your _____, which is of you kept back by _____, crieth: and the _____ of them which have reaped are entered into the ears of the _____ of sabaoth.

cries   labourers   Lord   fields   fraud

16 God's Provisions

1. 1 Kings 17:13–16
And Elijah said unto her, Fear not; go and do as thou hast said: but make me thereof a little cake first, and bring it unto me, and after make for thee and for thy _____. For thus saith the Lord God of _____, The barrel of meal shall not waste, neither shall the cruse of oil fail, until the day that the Lord sendeth rain upon the earth. And she went and did according to the saying of _____: and she, and he, and her _____, did eat many days. And the barrel of _____ wasted not, neither did the cruse of oil fail, according to the word of the Lord, which he spake by Elijah.

> meal   house   Elijah   Israel   son

2. Nehemiah 6:9
For they all made us _____, saying, Their _____ shall be _____ from the work, that it be not done. Now _____, O God, strengthen my hands.

> therefore   afraid   hands   weakened

3. Psalm 37:25
I have been _____, and now am _____; yet have I not seen the righteous forsaken, nor his _____ begging _____.

> old   bread   young   seed

4. Matthew 6:31–32

Therefore take no thought, saying, What shall we eat? or, What shall we drink? or, Wherewithal shall we be _____? (For after all these things do the _____ seek:) for your heavenly _____ knoweth that ye have need of all these _____.

Father things Gentiles clothed

5. Matthew 7:11

If ye then, being _____, know how to give good gifts unto your _____, how much more shall your _____ which is in _____ give good things to them that ask him?

heaven evil children Father

6. Luke 12:7

But even the very _____ of your _____ are all _____. Fear not therefore: ye are of more _____ than many _____.

value sparrows head hairs numbered

7. John 21:6

And he said unto them, _____ the _____ on the _____ side of the _____, and ye shall find. They cast therefore, and now they were not able to draw it for the multitude of _____.

net ship fishes cast right

8. 2 Corinthians 9:8

And God is able to make all _____ abound toward you; that ye, always having _____ _____ in all things, may _____ to every good _____.

> all   abound   work   grace   sufficiency

9. Philippians 4:19

But my _____ shall supply all your need according to his _____ in _____ by Christ _____.

> Jesus   God   riches   glory

17 Lending

1. Exodus 22:25

If thou lend _____ to any of my _____ that is poor by thee, _____ shalt not be to him as an usurer, neither shalt thou lay upon him _____.

> people   usury   money   thou

2. Leviticus 25:35–37

And if thy brother be _____ poor, and fallen in
_____ with thee; then thou shalt relieve him: yea,
though he be a stranger, or a _____; that he may
live with thee. Take thou no usury of him, or increase: but
fear thy God; that thy _____ may live with thee.
Thou shalt not give him thy _____ upon usury, nor
lend him thy _____ for increase.

> sojourner waxen decay victuals money brother

3. Deuteronomy 15:8

But thou shalt open thine _____ wide unto
him, and shalt surely lend him _____ for his
_____, in that which he _____.

> need hand wanteth sufficient

4. Deuteronomy 23:19–20

Thou shalt not _____ upon usury to thy
_____; usury of money, usury of victuals, usury
of any thing that is lent upon usury: Unto a _____
thou mayest lend upon usury; but unto thy brother thou
shalt not lend upon usury: that the LORD thy _____
may _____ thee in all that thou settest thine
_____ to in the land whither thou goest to possess it.

> stranger God bless brother lend hand

5. Deuteronomy 24:10

When thou dost _____ thy _____ any
thing, thou shalt not go into his _____ to fetch his
_____.

| pledge   house   brother   lend |

6. Psalm 15:5

He that putteth not out his _____ to
_____, nor taketh reward against the
_____. He that doeth these _____ shall
never be _____.

| things   moved   usury   money   innocent |

7. Psalm 37:26

_____ is ever _____, and lendeth; and his
_____ is _____.

| merciful   seed   blessed   he |

8. Psalm 112:5

A good _____ _____ favour,
and _____: he will guide his affairs with
_____.

| lendeth   discretion   sheweth   man |

9. Proverbs 3:27–28

Withhold not good from them to whom it is due, when it is in the _____ of thine _____ to do it. Say not unto thy _____, Go, and come again, and to morrow I will give; when thou hast it by _____.

> neighbour   power   thee   hand

10. Proverbs 28:8

He that by _____ and unjust gain _____ his _____, he shall gather it for him that will pity the _____.

> poor   increaseth   substance   usury

11. Matthew 5:42

Give to him that _____ _____, and from him that would _____ of thee turn not _____ away.

> thou   asketh   borrow   thee

12. Luke 6:35

But love ye your _____, and do good, and lend, hoping for _____ again; and your reward shall be _____, and ye shall be the _____ of the _____: for he is kind unto the unthankful and to the _____.

> Highest   children   evil   enemies   great   nothing

18 Being Truly Prosperous

1. Genesis 26:12

Then Isaac sowed in that _____, and received in the same _____ an _____: and the LORD _____ him.

> land   year   blessed   hundredfold

2. Genesis 39:3

And his _____ saw that the LORD was with him, and that the _____ made all that he did to _____ in his _____.

> LORD   hand   master   prosper

3. Deuteronomy 8:18

But thou shalt _____ the LORD thy God: for it is he that giveth thee _____ to get _____, that he may establish his _____ which he sware unto thy _____, as it is this day.

> fathers   wealth   power   remember   covenant

4. Deuteronomy 15:10

_____ shalt surely give him, and thine heart shall not be _____ when thou givest unto him: because that for this thing the LORD thy God shall _____ thee in all thy _____, and in all that thou puttest thine _____ unto.

> bless   works   grieved   thou   hand

5. Deuteronomy 24:19

When thou cuttest down thine _____ in thy field, and hast forgot a _____ in the field, thou shalt not go again to _____ it: it shall be for the stranger, for the fatherless, and for the widow: that the _____ thy God may bless thee in all the _____ of thine hands.

> harvest   work   fetch   Lord   sheaf

6. Deuteronomy 30:8–10

And thou shalt return and obey the voice of the Lord, and do all his commandments which I command thee this day. And the Lord thy God will make thee plenteous in every _____ of thine hand, in the fruit of thy body, and in the fruit of thy _____, and in the fruit of thy land, for good: for the Lord will again rejoice over thee for good, as he rejoiced over thy _____: If thou shalt hearken unto the _____ of the Lord thy God, to keep his _____ and his statutes which are written in this book of the law, and if thou turn unto the Lord thy God with all thine heart, and with all thy _____.

> commandments   soul   cattle   work   voice   fathers

7. Joshua 1:8

This book of the law shall not depart out of thy _____; but thou shalt meditate therein day and _____, that thou mayest observe to do according to all that is _____ therein: for then thou shalt make thy way prosperous, and then thou shalt have good _____.

> written   success   mouth   night

8. 1 Chronicles 22:12

Only the _____ give thee wisdom and understanding, and give thee _____ concerning Israel,
that thou mayest keep the _____ of the LORD thy
_____.

law God LORD charge

9. 2 Chronicles 31:20

And thus did _____ throughout all _____,
and wrought that which was good and right and truth before
the _____ his _____.

Judah LORD God Hezekiah

10. Psalm 1:1–3

Blessed is the man that walketh not in the counsel of the
_____, nor standeth in the way of sinners, nor
sitteth in the seat of the _____. But his delight is
in the law of the LORD; and in his law doth he meditate day
and night. And he shall be like a _____ planted by
the rivers of _____, that bringeth forth his fruit in
his season; his leaf also shall not wither; and whatsoever he
doeth shall _____.

ungodly tree prosper water scornful

11. Psalm 35:27

Let them shout for joy, and be glad, that favour my
_____ cause: yea, let them say continually, Let
the LORD be _____, which hath pleasure in the
_____ of his _____.

servant magnified righteous prosperity

12. Jeremiah 17:8

For he shall be as a _____ planted by the _____, and that spreadeth out her roots by the _____, and shall not see when heat cometh, but her leaf shall be _____; and shall not be careful in the year of _____, neither shall cease from yielding fruit.

green   drought   waters   tree   river

13. Malachi 3:10

Bring ye all the _____ into the storehouse, that there may be meat in mine _____, and prove me now herewith, saith the _____ of _____, if I will not open you the windows of _____, and pour you out a _____, that there shall not be room enough to receive it.

blessing   Lord   hosts   house   tithes   heaven

14. 3 John 1:2

_____, I wish above all things that thou mayest _____ and be in _____, even as thy _____ prospereth.

prosper   health   soul   beloved

19 Being a Good Steward over One's Money

1. Genesis 2:15

And the Lord God _____ the _____, and put him into the _____ of _____ to dress it and to _____ it.

> Eden   garden   man   keep   took

2. Deuteronomy 10:14

_____, the _____ and the heaven of _____ is the Lord's thy God, the _____ also, with all that therein is.

> heavens   earth   heaven   behold

3. Luke 12:42–44

And the Lord said, Who then is that faithful and wise _____, whom his lord shall make _____ over his _____, to give them their portion of _____ in due season? Blessed is that _____, whom his lord when he cometh shall find so doing. Of a truth I say unto you, that he will make him ruler over all that he hath.

> steward   ruler   household   meat   servant

4. Luke 12:47–48

And that _____, which knew his lord's will, and prepared not himself, neither did according to his will, shall be beaten with many stripes. But he that knew not, and did commit things worthy of _____, shall be _____ with few stripes. For unto _____ much is given, of him shall be much required: and to whom men have _____ much, of him they will ask the more.

> committed   stripes   servant   whomsoever   beaten

5. Luke 16:9–11

And I say unto you, Make to yourselves _____ of the mammon of unrighteousness; that, when ye fail, they may receive you into everlasting habitations. He that is faithful in that which is least is _____ also in much: and he that is _____ in the least is unjust also in much. If therefore ye have not been faithful in the unrighteous _____, who will commit to your trust the true _____?

> unjust   mammon   faithful   friends   riches

6. Romans 14:8

For whether we live, we live unto the Lord; and whether we _____, we die unto the _____: whether we _____ therefore, or die, we are the _____.

> Lord's   die   live   Lord

20 Saving

1. Proverbs 21:5

The _____ of the diligent _____ only to plenteousness; but of every one that is _____ only to _____.

hasty   thoughts   tend   want

2. Proverbs 21:20

There is _____ to be desired and _____ in the dwelling of the _____; but a foolish man _____ it up.

oil   treasure   wise   spendeth

3. Proverbs 27:12

A _____ man foreseeth the _____, and hideth himself; but the _____ pass on, and are _____.

evil   prudent   punished   simple

4. Proverbs 30:25

The ants are a _____ not strong, yet they prepare their meat in the _____.

summer   people

5. 1 Corinthians 16:2

Upon the first _____ of the _____ let every one of you lay by him in store, as _____ hath prospered him, that there be no _____ when I come.

> God   week   day   gatherings

21 **Tithing**

1. Genesis 14:20

And blessed be the most high _____, which hath delivered _____ enemies into thy _____. And he gave him _____ of all.

> thine   tithes   God   hand

2. Genesis 28:20–22

And _____ vowed a vow, saying, If God will be with me, and will keep me in this way that I go, and will give me _____ to eat, and raiment to put on, So that I come again to my father's _____ in peace; then shall the LORD be my God: And this stone, which I have set for a _____, shall be God's house: and of all that thou shalt give me I will surely give the _____ unto thee.

> house   tenth   bread   Jacob   pillar

3. Exodus 23:19

The first of the _____ of thy _____ thou shalt bring into the _____ of the LORD thy God. Thou shalt not seethe a _____ in his mother's _____.

> milk land firstfruits house kid

4. Leviticus 27:30

And all the _____ of the _____, whether of the _____ of the land, or of the fruit of the tree, is the LORD's: it is holy unto the _____.

> land seed LORD tithe

5. Numbers 18:26

Thus speak unto the _____, and say unto them, When ye take of the children of _____ the tithes which I have given you from them for your _____, then ye shall offer up an heave offering of it for the LORD, even a tenth part of the _____.

> tithe Levites Israel inheritance

6. Deuteronomy 14:22–23

Thou shalt truly _____ all the increase of thy seed, that the field bringeth forth _____ by year. And thou shalt eat before the LORD thy God, in the place which he shall choose to place his _____ there, the tithe of thy _____, of thy wine, and of thine oil, and the _____ of thy herds and of thy _____; that thou mayest learn to fear the LORD thy God always.

> year tithe flocks firstlings corn name

7. Deuteronomy 14:28

At the end of _____ _____ thou
shalt bring forth all the tithe of thine _____
the same _____, and shalt lay it up within thy
_____.

> increase   three   years   gates   year

8. Deuteronomy 26:12

When thou hast made an end of _____ all the
tithes of thine increase the third year, which is the year
of tithing, and hast given it unto the _____,
the _____, the _____, and the
_____, that they may eat within thy gates, and be
filled.

> widow   stranger   fatherless   Levite   tithing

9. 2 Chronicles 31:5

And as soon as the _____ came abroad, the children of _____ brought in abundance the firstfruits
of corn, _____, and oil, and honey, and of all the
increase of the field; and the _____ of all things
brought they in _____.

> abundantly   tithe   commandment   Israel   wine

10. Nehemiah 10:38

And the priest the son of _____ shall be with the
_____, when the Levites take _____:
and the Levites shall bring up the tithe of the tithes unto
the _____ of our God, to the chambers, into the
_____ house.

> treasure   Aaron   Levites   house   tithes

11. Proverbs 3:9–10

Honour the _____ with thy substance, and
with the firstfruits of all thine increase: So shall thy
_____ be filled with _____, and thy
presses shall burst out with new _____.

plenty LORD wine barns

12. Ezekiel 44:30

And the first of all the _____ of all things, and
every oblation of all, of every sort of your oblations, shall
be the priest's: ye shall also give unto the _____
the first of your _____, that he may cause the
_____ to rest in thine house.

priest dough firstfruits blessing

13. Amos 4:4

Come to _____, and transgress; at Gilgal multiply
_____; and bring your _____ every morn-
ing, and your _____ after three years.

transgression sacrifices Bethel tithes

14. Malachi 3:8

Will a man _____ God? Yet ye have _____
me. But ye say, Wherein have we robbed _____? In
_____ and _____.

robbed rob offerings tithes thee

15. Matthew 23:23

Woe unto you, scribes and _____, hypocrites! for ye pay tithe of mint and anise and _____, and have omitted the _____ matters of the law, _____, mercy, and faith: these ought ye to have done, and not to leave the other _____.

cummin   undone   weightier   Pharisees   judgment

16. 1 Corinthians 16:1–2

Now concerning the collection for the _____, as I have given order to the _____ of _____, even so do ye. Upon the first day of the _____ let every one of you lay by him in store, as _____ hath prospered him, that there be no gatherings when I come.

God   saints   churches   Galatia   week

17. Hebrews 7:4

Now consider how great this _____ was, unto whom even the _____ _____ gave the tenth of the _____.

spoils   patriarch   man   Abraham

Specialized Multiple-Choice Trivia

Next is a large array of multiple-choice trivia by topic. Give yourself 1 point for each correct answer, and as always, you may repeat any or all of the quizzes as many times as necessary.

Take your time. This is not a race, and your ability to retain this information is greatly enhanced if you meditate on each answer.

22 | All about Food

1. Who ate locusts in the wilderness?

A. Matthew

B. Paul

C. John the Baptist

D. Peter

2. Who traded his birthright for his brother's bread and lentil stew?

A. Jacob

B. David

C. Joseph

D. Esau

3. Who had a baker who baked pastries for him?

A. The pharaoh in Moses's time

B. The pharaoh in Joseph's time

C. Samson

D. Gideon

4. Who was tricked when his non-hairy son dressed in hairy gloves and presented him with a meal?

A. Jacob

B. Esau

C. Isaac

D. Israel

5. What did Ezekiel's scroll taste like?

A. Candy

B. Honey

C. Fish

D. Wafers

6. What judge of Israel prepared a delicious meal for an angel?

   A. Gideon

   B. Samson

   C. Ehud

   D. Deborah

7. What book of the Bible describes Canaan as a land flowing with milk and honey?

   A. Genesis

   B. Exodus

   C. Leviticus

   D. Judges

8. What animal was killed for food when the prodigal son returned home?

   A. A hog

   B. A rooster

   C. A turkey

   D. The fatted calf

9. Where did the Hebrews feast on cucumbers, melons, leeks, onions, and garlic?

   A. Jerusalem

   B. Bethlehem

   C. Egypt

   D. Gilead

10. Who ate honey out of a lion's carcass?

   A. David

   B. Elijah

   C. Saul

   D. Samson

11. What prophet made deadly stew edible again?

A. Elijah

B. Elisha

C. Jeremiah

D. Obadiah

12. What miraculous food fed the Israelites in the desert?

A. Potatoes

B. Manna

C. Fish

D. Five loaves of bread

23 From Sweet to Bitter

1. Who ate a book that was originally sweet but turned bitter?

A. Peter

B. Mark

C. Thomas

D. John

2. Who presented a riddle about finding something sweet in a lion's carcass?

A. Elijah

B. Elisha

C. Samson

D. Joel

3. According to Proverbs, what kind of bread is sweet to a man?

   A. Bread of deceit

   B. Bread of idleness

   C. Bread of comfort

   D. Bread of humbleness

4. What kind of grape sets the children's teeth on edge, according to Jeremiah?

   A. Red

   B. Green

   C. Sour

   D. Sweet

5. What type of herbs were the Israelites supposed to eat with the Passover meal?

   A. None

   B. Sweet herbs

   C. Bitter herbs

   D. Sour herbs

6. According to Proverbs, what kind of water is sweet?

   A. Purified water

   B. Rain water

   C. River water

   D. Stolen water

7. What did Moses do to make the bitter waters of Marah drinkable?

   A. He threw a piece of wood in the water.

   B. He poured some honey in the water.

   C. He prayed over the water.

   D. He fasted several days.

8. After his resurrection, what did Jesus say his followers would be able to drink?

   A. Juice

   B. Milk

   C. Water

   D. Poison

9. What strange thing did Moses make the people of Israel drink?

   A. Cane sugar

   B. Honey

   C. Silver

   D. Gold dust

10. According to Proverbs, what sort of person thinks bitter things are sweet?

    A. A conceited person

    B. A prideful person

    C. A hungry person

    D. A loving person

24 Kiddie Land

1. Who was the first child mentioned in the Bible?

   A. Cain

   B. Abel

   C. Seth

   D. Ham

2. Who was Noah's youngest son?

   A. Shem

   B. Japheth

   C. Ham

   D. Benjamin

3. What king was the youngest of eight brothers?

   A. Saul

   B. David

   C. Solomon

   D. Ahab

4. Who was the youngest son of Joseph?

   A. Manasseh

   B. Ephraim

   C. Malachi

   D. Jair

5. Who of the following was not a son of Adam?

   A. Cain

   B. Abel

   C. Seth

   D. Ahab

6. Who died giving birth to Benjamin?

   A. Rebekah

   B. Rachel

   C. Rhoda

   D. Rahab

7. What judge had seventy sons?

   A. Samson

   B. Gideon

   C. Deborah

   D. Samuel

8. What king of Judah had twenty-eight sons and sixty daughters?

   A. Rehoboam

   B. David

   C. Solomon

   D. Saul

9. Who advised young Christians to stop thinking as children think?

   A. Peter

   B. Paul

   C. Pilate

   D. John

10. What king was severely distressed over the death of his wayward son?

    A. Saul

    B. Solomon

    C. David

    D. Heman

25　Did You Know? (Set 4)

Prepare to be amazed by the following Bible facts.

- Approximately forty men wrote the Bible over a sixteen-hundred-year period. The time of the writing dates from 1500 BC to approximately AD 100.
- The Red Sea was not the only waterway parted by God. He also parted the Jordan River for Elijah and Elisha (2 Kings 2:7–9).

- Pontius Pilate and King Herod were bitter enemies until they became friends during Jesus's persecution (Luke 23:12).
- In the Gospels, Jesus is called the "Son of man" over seventy-five times.
- David kept Goliath's armor in his tent as a souvenir after slaying him (1 Samuel 17:54).
- Abraham was not circumcised until he was ninety-nine years old (Genesis 17:24).
- The place where Jesus was crucified, "the place of a skull," contained a garden (John 19:17–18, 41).

26 That Makes Scents

1. What aromatic substance was brought to the baby Jesus?
   A. Ginger
   B. Frankincense
   C. Cinnamon
   D. Palm leaves
2. Whose harem contained women who were purified with various perfumes?
   A. King Herod
   B. King Ahaz
   C. King Josiah
   D. King Ahasuerus

3. In the Gospel of John, who anointed Jesus's feet with spike-nard, an expensive ointment?

    A. Mary Magdalene

    B. Mary, mother of Jesus

    C. Mary, sister of Lazarus

    D. Mary, a nurse

4. In the Gospel of Luke, where was Jesus when a sinful woman poured an alabaster jar of perfume on his feet?

    A. At the home of Simon the Pharisee

    B. At Peter's house

    C. At the home of John and James

    D. In Bethlehem

5. What book of the Bible mentions a woman using spikenard, calamus, and various perfumes?

    A. Proverbs

    B. Psalms

    C. Song of Solomon

    D. Esther

6. Who perfumed her bed with myrrh, aloes, and cinnamon?

    A. The bride

    B. The harlot

    C. The mother

    D. The virtuous woman

7. What man used myrrh and frankincense as perfumes?

    A. Solomon

    B. David

    C. Saul

    D. Jonathan

8. What prophet refused to use anointing oils during mourning?

   A. Elijah

   B. Daniel

   C. Jonah

   D. Joel

9. According to the book of Proverbs, ointment and perfume do what?

   A. Help people to love everybody

   B. Rejoice the heart

   C. Make peace in the valley

   D. Bring laughter

10. What two prophets denounced women applying makeup?

   A. Elijah and Elisha

   B. Jonah and Joel

   C. Samuel and Josiah

   D. Jeremiah and Ezekiel

27 Wedding Bells

1. Who was the first man mentioned in the Bible to have more than one wife?

   A. Adam

   B. Lamech

   C. Moses

   D. Seth

2. Who married both Rachel and Leah?

    A. Lamech

    B. Abdon

    C. Jotham

    D. Jacob

3. Whose father's wives were named Hannah and Peninnah?

    A. Jacob's

    B. Samuel's

    C. Abraham's

    D. Isaac's

4. What king was married to Ahinoam?

    A. Josiah

    B. Saul

    C. David

    D. Solomon

5. Mahlon and Boaz were the husbands of what woman?

    A. Orpah

    B. Ruth

    C. Naomi

    D. Rachel

6. Who married two of Judah's sons?

    A. Rachel

    B. Leah

    C. Rebekah

    D. Tamar

7. What king of Judah had fourteen wives?

    A. Abijah

    B. Aaron

    C. Uzziah

    D. Saul

8. What judge of Israel surrendered his Philistine wife to a friend?

   A. Samson

   B. Othniel

   C. Ehud

   D. Gideon

28 Farming

1. Who planted the first garden?

   A. Adam

   B. Solomon

   C. Noah

   D. God

2. Who of the following was a farmer?

   A. Jacob

   B. Job

   C. Paul

   D. Stephen

3. What king planted many vineyards, gardens, and orchards?

   A. Pharaoh

   B. David

   C. Saul

   D. Solomon

4. What judge was also a farmer of grain?

  A. Gideon

  B. Othniel

  C. Deborah

  D. Joel

5. Who was the first man to plant a vineyard?

  A. Adam

  B. Cain

  C. Enoch

  D. Noah

6. What farmer and ancestor of David married a Moabite woman?

  A. Elimelech

  B. Ahaziah

  C. Boaz

  D. Ehud

7. Who was a farmer in Gerar and received a hundredfold harvest?

  A. Jacob

  B. Isaac

  C. Abraham

  D. Noah

8. What king of Judah enjoyed farming?

  A. Uzziah

  B. Ahaziah

  C. Amaziah

  D. Uriah

9. Who had a vineyard that was coveted by Ahab?

A. Naaman

B. Naboth

C. Obadiah

D. Omri

10. David commanded Ziba to farm for what lame man?

A. Naaman

B. Hezekiah

C. Mephibosheth

D. Jeroboam

29 Rulers

1. What king made a famous ruling that involved cutting a baby in two?

A. David

B. Pharaoh

C. Solomon

D. Saul

2. Who was the first king to reign in Jerusalem?

A. Saul

B. David

C. Ahasuerus

D. Pharaoh

3. What wicked ruler ordered the infant boys of Bethlehem to be slaughtered?

   A. Pharaoh

   B. Saul

   C. Archelaus

   D. Herod

4. What ruler ordered that Daniel be thrown into the lions' den?

   A. Nebuchadnezzar

   B. Belshazzar

   C. Darius

   D. Ahasuerus

5. What king of Judah was hobbled by a foot disease in his old age?

   A. Asa

   B. Rehoboam

   C. Abijah

   D. Jehoshaphat

6. What young shepherd boy was anointed by Samuel in front of his brothers?

   A. Solomon

   B. David

   C. Joseph

   D. Josiah

7. What imprisoned man interpreted the dreams of the Egyptian pharaoh?

   A. Jacob

   B. Moses

   C. Joseph

   D. Reuben

8. What wise king became allies with Egypt when he married Pharaoh's daughter?

   A. Jeroboam II

   B. Solomon

   C. Menahem

   D. Saul

9. What man led in the conquering of thirty-one kings and their empires?

   A. Samson

   B. David

   C. Joshua

   D. Elisha

10. What king of Moab commanded that the prophet Balaam go and curse Israel?

    A. Balak

    B. Ahaziah

    C. Pharaoh

    D. Saul

11. What son of Gideon (Jerubbaal) became king in Shechem?

    A. Joash

    B. Ezekiel

    C. Abimelech

    D. Abiezer

12. What king of the Amalekites was captured by Saul and severed into pieces by Samuel?

    A. Omri

    B. Agag

    C. Jehu

    D. Ahab

13. David sought refuge with what Philistine king after fleeing from Saul?

A. Achish

B. Saul

C. Hoshea

D. Elah

30 The Apostles

1. What was Peter's original name?

A. Philip

B. Levi

C. Simon

D. Epaphras

2. Who was with Jesus at the transfiguration?

A. Matthew

B. John

C. Mark

D. Luke

3. Who healed Aeneas, a paralytic?

A. Paul

B. Stephen

C. Peter

D. Jesus

4. Who brought Greeks to Jesus?

A. Andrew

B. James

C. Thaddaeus

D. Matthew

31 In the Military

1. Who was sleeping between two soldiers when miraculously rescued from prison?

A. Paul

B. John

C. Peter

D. Timothy

2. What leper commanded Syrian troops?

A. Nathan

B. Nathanael

C. Nethaniah

D. Naaman

3. Where was Jesus when a Roman officer asked him to heal his faithful servant?

A. Bethsaida

B. Capernaum

C. Cana

D. Tiberias

4. What Roman soldier was kind to Paul on Paul's voyage to Rome?

    A. Pontius

    B. Julius

    C. Onesimus

    D. Felix

5. What Israelite soldier gave Joshua an enthusiastic report about the land of Canaan?

    A. Jephunneh

    B. Othniel

    C. Caleb

    D. Nun

6. What Hittite soldier was put on the front lines of battle specifically to allow David to have his widow?

    A. Amaziah

    B. Uzziah

    C. Uriah

    D. Ahaziah

7. What soldier supported David during Absalom's rebellion?

    A. Goliath

    B. Ittai

    C. Obededom

    D. Zeruiah

8. What soldier led a revolt against King Elah and made himself the new king?

    A. Zichri

    B. Zophar

    C. Zimri

    D. Zerubbabel

9. Who commanded the rebel army when Absalom rebelled against David?

A. Ahasuerus

B. Amasa

C. Amram

D. Aristarchus

32 Women and Rulers

1. Who became David's wife and gave him a son named Solomon?

A. Jezebel

B. Abigail

C. Bathsheba

D. Delilah

2. What king of Israel had Rizpah as his concubine?

A. David

B. Saul

C. Solomon

D. Jeroboam

3. Who plotted to have John the Baptist beheaded?

A. Euodias

B. Eunice

C. Herodias

D. Hannah

4. What princess led Ahab into the depths of idolatry?

A. Salome

B. Jezebel

C. Bithiah

D. Serah

5. What queen traveled a great distance to meet Solomon face-to-face?

A. Queen Vashti

B. Queen Esther

C. The queen of Sheba

D. Queen Maachah

6. Who was replaced by a foreign woman after defying her royal husband?

A. Esther

B. Deborah

C. Vashti

D. Claudia

7. After Nabal died, who became David's wife?

A. Bathsheba

B. Abigail

C. Baara

D. Abijah

8. Who was ousted as queen mother for making a false idol?

A. Maachah

B. Herodias

C. Asenath

D. Cleopatra

9. Philip witnessed to an Ethiopian eunuch who was the servant of what queen?

    A. Queen Herodias

    B. Queen Candace

    C. Queen Nitocris

    D. Queen Esther

10. What daughter of Ahab tried to destroy the entire line of Judah?

    A. Jemima

    B. Myrrina

    C. Huldah

    D. Athaliah

33 Hair Apparent

1. What famous figure never had a haircut until his mistress had his head shaved?

    A. Othniel

    B. Barak

    C. Samson

    D. Joseph

2. What apostle, along with four other men, purified himself by shaving his head?

    A. Joseph

    B. Paul

    C. Jonathan

    D. James

3. What king of Babylon once lived in the wilderness and let his hair grow wild?

   A. Daniel

   B. Nebuchadnezzar

   C. Elijah

   D. Naaman

4. Who is mentioned in the book of Genesis as being very hairy?

   A. Noah

   B. Abraham

   C. Esau

   D. Joseph

5. What prophet was described as a very hairy man?

   A. Elisha

   B. Hosea

   C. Elijah

   D. Amos

6. What man, stricken by grief, shaved his head after he learned his children had been killed?

   A. Noah

   B. Naaman

   C. David

   D. Job

7. Who was forbidden to "round the corners of your heads"?

   A. Greeks

   B. Chaldeans

   C. The children of Israel

   D. Egyptians

8. Who was the only man in the Bible referred to as being naturally bald?

   A. Elijah

   B. Jacob

   C. Elisha

   D. Esau

9. What type of person had to shave all his hair twice, six days apart?

   A. An epileptic

   B. A blind man

   C. A leper

   D. A paralytic

10. What type of people could neither shave their heads nor let their hair grow long?

    A. Pharisees

    B. Prophets

    C. Levite priests

    D. Scribes

11. God told what prophet to shave his head and beard?

    A. Isaiah

    B. Jeremiah

    C. Ezekiel

    D. Daniel

34 Anointment

1. Who was anointed by the Holy Ghost?

    A. Moses

    B. Peter

    C. Joseph

    D. Jesus

2. Who anointed the tabernacle with oil?

    A. Aaron

    B. Bezaleel

    C. Moses

    D. Solomon

3. Who anointed a stone before dedicating it to God?

    A. Esau

    B. Jacob

    C. Aaron

    D. Joseph

4. Who told the early Christians that God had "given the earnest of the Spirit in our hearts"?

    A. Peter

    B. John

    C. James

    D. Paul

5. What man and his sons were anointed by Moses with the blood of a ram?

    A. Elijah and his sons

    B. Caleb and his sons

    C. Aaron and his sons

    D. Joshua and his sons

6. What well-respected judge anointed Saul?

   A. David

   B. Deborah

   C. Othniel

   D. Samuel

7. According to James, who should anoint a sick believer with oil?

   A. The saved

   B. The deacons

   C. The elders

   D. The scribes

8. What king of Persia was regarded to be God's anointed one?

   A. Ahasuerus

   B. Cyrus

   C. Alexander

   D. Belshazzar

9. What priest anointed Solomon king?

   A. Aaron

   B. Zadok

   C. Melchisedec

   D. Joshua

35 | The Swift

1. What boy raced to the Philistine camp to challenge the feared Philistine warrior?

A. Samuel

B. Jesus

C. David

D. Solomon

2. What height-challenged man ran to see Jesus but could not because he was too short?

A. Bartimaeus

B. Peter

C. Zacchaeus

D. John

3. What combative man ran to meet his brother and kissed him after a long time apart?

A. Esau

B. Benjamin

C. James

D. Abel

4. What prophet outran a king's chariot and its team of horses?

A. Isaiah

B. Jeremiah

C. Elijah

D. Zedekiah

5. In the plains of Mamre, who ran to meet the Lord?

A. Noah

B. Abraham

C. Moses

D. Joshua

6. What man ran to meet Abraham's servant at the well?

    A. Isaac

    B. Jacob

    C. Laban

    D. Abimelech

7. Who sent Cushi to run to David with the news of Absalom's death?

    A. Joab

    B. Jonathan

    C. Joram

    D. Jethro

8. What encroacher to the throne of Israel found fifty men to run before him?

    A. Adonijah

    B. Samson

    C. Zerubbabel

    D. David

9. What man, a servant of the prophet Elisha, ran to meet the woman of Shunem?

    A. Shemariah

    B. Nebajoth

    C. Caleb

    D. Gehazi

36 Special Women

1. Who was the only female judge of Israel?

    A. Deborah

    B. Sarah

    C. Rebekah

    D. Ruth

2. What cousin of Mary gave birth to John the Baptist?

    A. Elisabeth

    B. Anna

    C. Bernice

    D. Herodias

3. What prophetess was the sister of Moses and Aaron?

    A. Sarah

    B. Miriam

    C. Deborah

    D. Rebekah

4. What Jewish girl married an emperor and helped save her people from certain extermination?

    A. Ruth

    B. Naomi

    C. Esther

    D. Deborah

5. What deceitful princess of the Zidonians married Ahab?

    A. Ruth

    B. Bathsheba

    C. Esther

    D. Jezebel

6. What wife of David was once married to Nabal?

A. Hildah

B. Azubah

C. Abigail

D. Ahinoam

7. What harlot helped save the lives of Joshua's spies?

A. Bathsheba

B. Leah

C. Hodiah

D. Rahab

8. What wife of David was the mother of the disobedient Adonijah?

A. Abigail

B. Bathsheba

C. Michal

D. Haggith

9. Who protected the corpses of her slaughtered children from birds and various animals?

A. Rizpah

B. Baara

C. Bathsheba

D. Reumah

10. What prophetess consoled the king while severely criticizing the people of Judah?

A. Deborah

B. Naomi

C. Huldah

D. Miriam

37 | Fly High

1. What cannot be tamed even though all birds can be tamed, according to James?

A. The mind

B. The tongue

C. The heart

D. The soul

2. The Holy Spirit took the form of what bird at Jesus's baptism?

A. Raven

B. Pigeon

C. Dove

D. Eagle

3. How many of each species of bird was Noah commanded to take on to the ark?

A. 1

B. 3

C. 5

D. 7

4. Who had a vision that featured a woman with eagle's wings flying to the desert?

A. John

B. Paul

C. James

D. Peter

5. What bird was supplied in abundance to feed the Israelites in the wilderness?

   A. Eagle

   B. Quail

   C. Dove

   D. Raven

6. What parable of Jesus featured greedy birds?

   A. The tares

   B. The prodigal son

   C. The sower

   D. The great supper

38 What's That I Hear?

1. What apostle spoke to the Pentecost crowd in a loud voice?

   A. Peter

   B. Stephen

   C. John

   D. Judas

2. Who heard a voice talking of the fall of Babylon?

   A. John

   B. Barnabas

   C. Bartholomew

   D. Bildad

3. "This is my beloved Son, in whom I am well pleased" was spoken at what important event?

    A. Paul's conversion

    B. Jesus's baptism

    C. Peter's release from jail

    D. Jesus's ascension

4. Who heard the voice of those who had been slaughtered for proclaiming God's Word?

    A. Paul

    B. Elam

    C. John

    D. Caleb

5. Who heard the voice of God after he ran away from Queen Jezebel?

    A. Elisha

    B. David

    C. Elijah

    D. Gomer

6. What boy was sleeping near the ark of the covenant when he heard the voice of God?

    A. David

    B. Obededom

    C. Amaziah

    D. Samuel

7. What trees are broken by the power of God's voice, according to the book of Psalms?

    A. Sycamore trees

    B. Fig trees

    C. Cedars of Lebanon

    D. Lilies of the field

8. Whom did Isaiah tell that the king of Assyria had raised his voice up against God?

   A. Zechariah

   B. Hophni

   C. Zebediah

   D. Hezekiah

9. Who cried out upon seeing a vision of Samuel?

   A. Samuel's mother, Hannah

   B. Elkanah

   C. The witch of Endor

   D. King Saul

39 Did You Know? (Set 5)

Here are more facts for the Bible brilliant.

- The apostle Paul spoke both Greek and Hebrew (Acts 21:37–40).
- God once gave Moses leprosy for a short time (Exodus 4:6–7).
- The devastating earthquake mentioned in Amos 1:1 has been verified by modern geologists.
- Nowhere in the Bible does it specifically state or imply that Mary Magdalene was a prostitute.
- If one goes by the total number of words, Luke wrote more of the New Testament than Paul did.
- Moses could not have written the last chapter of Deuteronomy because he was dead. Joshua is thought to have finished the book.

40 The Story of Joseph

1. How many of Joseph's brothers traveled to Egypt to buy grain?

   A. 12

   B. 10

   C. 11

   D. 6

2. Which brother of Joseph did not go down to buy grain in Egypt?

   A. Reuben

   B. Benjamin

   C. Levi

   D. Judah

3. How many days did Joseph keep his brothers in prison?

   A. 3

   B. 14

   C. 20

   D. 1

4. Which of Joseph's brothers did Joseph keep tied up until Benjamin was brought back?

   A. Reuben

   B. Manasseh

   C. Levi

   D. Simeon

5. What did Joseph command to be placed in his brothers' sacks along with grain?

   A. Money

   B. Manna

   C. Quails

   D. Sword

6. When Joseph's brothers returned, what did Joseph command to be placed in Benjamin's sack?

   A. Golden candlestick

   B. Silver cup

   C. Bronze laver

   D. Golden ring

7. What did Joseph say the man who was found in possession of the silver cup would become?

   A. His successor

   B. His friend

   C. His servant

   D. His betrayer

8. During the seven years of famine, Joseph let his father and brothers dwell in what land?

   A. Hushim

   B. Goshen

   C. Beulah

   D. Moab

9. What did Pharaoh tell Joseph that his father and his household should eat?

   A. Milk and honeycomb

   B. From the fat of the land

   C. Manna

   D. Whatever they could find

10. How old was Joseph when he died?

    A. 99 years old

    B. 100 years old

    C. 110 years old

    D. 120 years old

11. What did Joseph name his first son?

    A. Jacob

    B. Ephraim

    C. Benjamin

    D. Manasseh

12. How many pieces of silver did Joseph give to his brother Benjamin?

    A. 100

    B. 1,000

    C. 300

    D. 3,000

Have a Laugh

1. Who was laughed at for saying that a dead girl was only asleep?

    A. Paul

    B. Jesus

    C. Peter

    D. Jairus

2. What elderly man laughed at God's promise that he would father a child in his old age?

    A. Noah

    B. Methuselah

    C. Abraham

    D. Saul

3. Who danced with great enthusiasm when the ark of the covenant was brought to Jerusalem?

A. David

B. Solomon

C. Obed

D. Uzziah

4. Who laughed when told that she would bear a son in her old age?

A. Rebekah

B. Anna

C. Leah

D. Sarah

5. After the exodus, the Israelites danced in front of what graven image?

A. A molten calf

B. Baal

C. A dual-horned unicorn

D. The Semel carved image

6. What elderly woman said, "God hath made me to laugh, so that all that hear will laugh with me"?

A. Eve

B. Rebekah

C. Leah

D. Sarah

7. In the Beatitudes, to whom did Jesus promise laughter?

A. Those who mourn

B. Those who are sad

C. Those who weep

D. Those who hunger

8. Whose daughter danced after his victory over the Ammonites?

   A. Jacob's

   B. Job's

   C. Jochebed's

   D. Jephthah's

9. Who was preoccupied with dancing when David caught them?

   A. Moabites

   B. Canaanites

   C. Amalekites

   D. Philistines

10. Who laughed when he learned of Nehemiah's plans to re-build Jerusalem?

    A. Sanballat

    B. Eliashib

    C. Shallum

    D. Benaiah

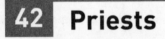

42 Priests

1. What severe penalty was handed out in Israel for disobeying a priest?

   A. Imprisonment

   B. Daily confession for a year

   C. Death

   D. Daily offering of a badger for a year

2. What was etched on the twelve stones in the high priest's breastplate?

   A. The names of the kings of Israel

   B. The names of the tribes of Israel

   C. Elohim

   D. Yahweh

3. What priest was said to have had no mother or father?

   A. Ezekiel

   B. Melchisedec

   C. Joshua

   D. Ananias

4. What priest was called "King of peace"?

   A. Zacharias

   B. Melchisedec

   C. Zadok

   D. Ezra

5. What priest chastised a woman because he thought she had been drinking at the tabernacle?

   A. Eli

   B. Abiathar

   C. Joshua

   D. Phinehas

6. What king ousted all the priests who had been appointed to serve pagan gods?

   A. David

   B. Jehu

   C. Shallum

   D. Josiah

7. What greedy priest was infamous for keeping the sacrificial meat all to himself?

   A. Ahimelech

   B. Aaron

   C. Phinehas

   D. Caiaphas

8. What priest located in Midian trained Moses in how to administer justice among the Hebrews?

   A. Aaron

   B. Jethro

   C. Aleazar

   D. Eli

43 Lions' Den

1. Who saw a creature resembling a lion near the throne of God?

   A. Moses

   B. Jonathan

   C. John

   D. Samuel

2. Who envisioned a lion with eagle's wings?

   A. Jeremiah

   B. Amos

   C. Haggai

   D. Daniel

3. Who claimed to have grabbed a lion by the throat and pummeled him to death?

A. King Hiram

B. King Nebuchadnezzar

C. King David

D. King Zimri

4. What person is like a ravenous lion, according to 1 Peter?

A. The devil

B. Judas

C. Herod

D. Elymas

5. Who ripped a lion apart with his bare hands?

A. Joshua

B. Samson

C. Jacob

D. Ethan

6. What two men did David say were stronger than lions?

A. Jacob and Joseph

B. Saul and Jonathan

C. Noah and Ham

D. Abraham and Isaac

7. What prophet had a vision of a creature with a lion's face as one of its four sides?

A. Isaiah

B. Jeremiah

C. Ezekiel

D. Micah

8. What soldier in David's army killed a lion in a pit on a snowy day?

A. Joab

B. Uriah

C. Shimei

D. Benaiah

44 Did You Know? (Set 6)

Ready for more astonishing facts? Help yourself.

- In the early thirteenth century, Archbishop Stephen Langton developed a system for dividing the Bible into chapters.
- At the grand dedication of God's temple, Solomon had 22,000 oxen and 120,000 sheep sacrificed (1 Kings 8:62–63).
- After the Israelites destroyed the temple of Baal, they used it as a communal latrine (draughthouse) (2 Kings 10:26–27).
- Luke, the only physician among the disciples, chronicled that as Jesus was praying in the Garden of Gethsemane before he was crucified, his extreme distress caused his perspiration to become like large drops of blood falling to the ground. This phenomenon is a medical condition called hematidrosis that only Luke the physician documented.
- Although dogs are mentioned in the Bible forty-one times, cats are not mentioned at all.
- God himself buried Moses in Moab, but no one knows precisely where (Deuteronomy 34:5–6).
- In Joshua 3:16, there is a town called Adam.

Scripture Fill in the Blanks

Fill in the blanks to complete the following Scripture passages. Give yourself 2 points for each correct passage.

45 | Scriptures on Assurance

1. Genesis 1:1

In the _____ God created the _____ and the _____.

2. Psalm 37:4

Delight _____ also in the _____: and he shall give thee the _____ of thine _____.

3. Isaiah 9:6

For unto us a _____ is born, unto us a son is given: and the _____ shall be upon his shoulder: and his name shall be called _____, Counsellor, The mighty God, The everlasting Father, The Prince of _____.

4. Isaiah 40:28

Hast thou not _____? hast thou not heard, that the _____ God, the LORD, the Creator of the ends of the earth, fainteth not, neither is _____? there is no searching of his understanding.

5. Jeremiah 29:11

For I know the _____ that I think toward you, saith the _____, thoughts of peace, and not of _____, to give you an expected end.

6. John 3:16

For God so _____ the _____, that he gave his only begotten _____, that whosoever believeth in him should not perish, but have everlasting _____.

7. John 15:7

If ye _____ in me, and my words abide in you, ye shall ask what ye _____, and it shall be done unto _____.

8. Romans 4:21

And being _____ persuaded that, what he had _____, he was able also to _____.

9. Romans 8:1

There is therefore now no _____ to them which are in Christ _____, who walk not after the flesh, but after the _____.

10. Romans 8:28

And we know that all things _____ together for _____ to them that _____ God, to them who are the called according to his _____.

11. 2 Corinthians 1:20

For all the _____ of God in him are yea, and in him _____, unto the _____ of God by us.

12. Ephesians 2:10

For we are his workmanship, created in Christ Jesus unto good _____, which God hath before _____ that we should walk in them.

13. Philippians 4:6–7

Be careful for _____; but in every thing by _____ and supplication with _____ let your requests be made known unto God. And the peace of God, which passeth all understanding, shall keep your hearts and _____ through Christ Jesus.

14. Philippians 4:19

But my God shall _____ all your need according to his _____ in _____ by Christ Jesus.

15. 2 Peter 1:4

Whereby are given unto us exceeding _____ and precious _____: that by these ye might be partakers of the divine _____, having escaped the corruption that is in the world through lust.

46 Scriptures on Salvation

1. John 14:6
Jesus saith unto him, I am the _____, the
truth, and the _____: no man cometh unto the
_____, but by me.

2. Romans 3:23
For all have _____, and come short of the
_____ of God.

3. Romans 6:23
For the wages of _____ is _____; but the
gift of God is eternal _____ through Jesus Christ
our Lord.

4. 2 Corinthians 5:17
Therefore if any man be in _____, he is a new
_____: old things are passed away; behold, all
things are become _____.

5. Ephesians 2:8–9
For by _____ are ye saved through
_____; and that not of yourselves: it is the gift of
God: Not of works, lest any man should _____.

6. Revelation 3:20
Behold, I stand at the _____, and _____:
if any man hear my _____, and open the door, I will
come in to him, and will sup with him, and he with me.

47 Scriptures on Security

1. Psalm 27:1

The _____ is my light and my _____;
whom shall I fear? the LORD is the strength of my life; of
whom shall I be _____?

2. Psalm 37:4

Delight _____ also in the LORD: and he shall give
thee the _____ of thine _____.

3. Proverbs 3:5–6

Trust in the _____ with all thine heart; and lean not
unto thine own _____. In all thy ways acknowledge
him, and he shall direct thy _____.

4. Isaiah 40:31

But they that _____ upon the _____
shall renew their strength; they shall mount up with wings as
eagles; they shall run, and not be _____; and they
shall walk, and not _____.

5. Jeremiah 29:11

For I know the thoughts that I think toward you, saith the
_____, thoughts of _____, and not of
_____, to give you an expected end.

6. Lamentations 3:22–23

It is of the LORD's _____ that we are not
_____, because his compassions fail not. They are
new every morning: great is thy _____.

7. Matthew 11:28–30

Come unto me, all ye that labour and are heavy
_____, and I will give you rest. Take my
_____ upon you, and learn of me; for I am
meek and lowly in _____: and ye shall find rest
unto your souls. For my yoke is easy, and my burden is
_____.

8. Luke 16:13

No _____ can serve two _____: for either he will hate the one, and love the other; or else he will hold to the one, and despise the other. Ye cannot serve _____ and mammon.

9. Acts 1:8

But ye shall receive _____, after that the Holy _____ is come upon you: and ye shall be witnesses unto me both in _____, and in all Judaea, and in Samaria, and unto the uttermost part of the _____.

10. Romans 8:28

And we know that all _____ work together for _____ to them that love God, to them who are the called according to his _____.

11. Romans 8:38–39

For I am persuaded, that neither _____, nor life, nor _____, nor principalities, nor powers, nor things present, nor things to come, Nor _____, nor depth, nor any other creature, shall be able to separate us from the love of God, which is in Christ Jesus our _____.

12. Romans 12:1

I beseech you therefore, _____, by the mercies of _____, that ye present your bodies a living _____, holy, acceptable unto God, which is your reasonable _____.

13. 1 Corinthians 15:58

Therefore, my beloved brethren, be ye stedfast, _____, always abounding in the _____ of the Lord, forasmuch as ye know that your labour is not in _____ in the Lord.

14. 2 Corinthians 4:18

While we _____ not at the things which are _____, but at the things which are not seen: for the things which are seen are _____; but the things which are not seen are _____.

15. 2 Corinthians 12:9

And he said unto me, My _____ is sufficient for _____: for my strength is made perfect in weakness. Most gladly therefore will I rather glory in my _____, that the power of Christ may rest upon me.

16. Galatians 2:20

I am _____ with Christ: nevertheless I live; yet not I, but Christ liveth in me: and the _____ which I now live in the flesh I live by the _____ of the Son of God, who loved me, and gave himself for me.

17. Galatians 5:22–23

But the _____ of the Spirit is love, joy, peace, _____, gentleness, goodness, _____, Meekness, temperance: against such there is no law.

18. Philippians 4:13

I can do all _____ through Christ which _____ me.

19. Colossians 3:23

And whatsoever ye do, do it _____, as to the Lord, and not unto _____.

20. Hebrews 12:1–2

Wherefore seeing we also are compassed about with so great a cloud of _____, let us lay aside every _____, and the sin which doth so easily beset us, and let us run with patience the race that is set before us, looking unto Jesus the author and finisher of our _____; who for the joy that was set before him endured the _____, despising the shame, and is set down at the right hand of the throne of God.

21. Hebrews 13:8

Jesus Christ the same _____, and to day, and for

_____.

22. James 1:22

But be ye _____ of the _____, and not

hearers only, deceiving your own _____.

23. James 4:7

_____ yourselves therefore to _____. Re-

sist the devil, and he will _____ from you.

24. 2 Peter 3:9

The _____ is not slack concerning his

_____, as some men count slackness; but is

longsuffering to us-ward, not willing that any should

_____, but that all should come to repentance.

25. 1 John 4:7–8

Beloved, let us _____ one another: for love is of

God; and every one that loveth is born of God, and knoweth

_____. He that loveth not knoweth not God; for

God is love.

48 Scriptures on Prayer

1. Psalm 19:14

Let the words of my _____, and the meditation of

my _____, be acceptable in thy sight, O LORD, my

_____, and my redeemer.

2. Psalm 50:14–15

Offer unto God _____; and pay thy vows unto the

most _____: And call upon me in the day of trou-

ble: I will deliver thee, and thou shalt _____ me.

3. Psalm 66:17

I cried unto him with my mouth, and he was extolled with my _____.

4. Psalm 95:2

Let us come before his presence with _____, and make a joyful _____ unto him with psalms.

5. Psalm 118:25

Save now, I beseech thee, O _____: O LORD, I beseech thee, send now _____.

6. Psalm 119:11

Thy _____ have I hid in mine _____, that I might not _____ against thee.

7. Psalm 119:105

Thy word is a _____ unto my _____, and a light unto my _____.

8. Psalm 122:6

_____ for the _____ of Jerusalem: they shall prosper that _____ thee.

9. Romans 10:1

Brethren, my heart's _____ and _____ to God for Israel is, that they might be _____.

10. Romans 10:13

For _____ shall call upon the _____ of the Lord shall be _____.

11. Romans 15:30

Now I beseech you, _____, for the Lord _____ Christ's sake, and for the _____ of the Spirit, that ye strive together with me in your _____ to God for me.

12. 1 Corinthians 1:4

I thank my God always on your _____, for the _____ of God which is given you by Jesus _____.

13. 1 Corinthians 14:15

What is it then? I will pray with the _____, and I will pray with the understanding also: I will sing with the spirit, and I will _____ with the understanding also.

14. 2 Corinthians 1:11

Ye also helping together by _____ for us, that for the _____ bestowed upon us by the means of many persons thanks may be given by many on our

_____.

15. Ephesians 6:18

_____ always with all prayer and _____ in the _____, and watching thereunto with all perseverance and supplication for all saints.

16. Philippians 1:3–4

I thank my _____ upon every _____ of you, always in every _____ of mine for you all making request with joy.

17. Colossians 1:3

We give thanks to God and the Father of our Lord Jesus Christ, _____ always for you.

18. 1 Thessalonians 5:17

_____ without ceasing.

19. 1 Thessalonians 5:18

In every thing give _____: for this is the will of God in Christ Jesus concerning _____.

20. James 1:6

But let him ask in _____, nothing wavering. For he that wavereth is like a wave of the _____ driven with the wind and _____.

21. James 5:13–14

Is any among you _____? let him _____. Is any merry? let him sing psalms. Is any sick among you? let him call for the elders of the _____; and let them pray over him, anointing him with _____ in the name of the Lord.

22. James 5:16

_____ your faults one to another, and _____ one for another, that ye may be _____. The effectual fervent prayer of a righteous man availeth much.

49 Scriptures on Temptation

1. Matthew 6:13
And _____ us not into _____, but deliver us from evil: For thine is the kingdom, and the power, and the _____, for ever. Amen.

2. Matthew 26:41
Watch and _____, that ye enter not into _____: the spirit indeed is willing, but the _____ is weak.

3. Luke 4:13
And when the _____ had ended all the _____, he departed from him for a _____.

4. Luke 11:4
And _____ us our sins; for we also forgive every one that is _____ to us. And lead us not into _____; but deliver us from evil.

5. Luke 22:40
And when he was at the _____, he said unto them, _____ that ye enter not into temptation.

6. 1 Corinthians 7:2

Nevertheless, to _____ fornication, let every man have his own _____, and let every woman have her own _____.

7. 1 Corinthians 10:13

There hath no _____ taken you but such as is common to _____: but God is _____, who will not suffer you to be tempted above that ye are able; but will with the temptation also make a way to _____, that ye may be able to bear it.

8. 1 Timothy 6:9

But they that will be _____ fall into temptation and a snare, and into many _____ and hurtful _____, which drown men in destruction and perdition.

50 Scriptures on Hope

1. Numbers 23:19

God is not a _____, that he should _____; neither the son of man, that he should repent: hath he said, and shall he not do it? or hath he spoken, and shall he not make it _____?

2. Job 13:15

Though he _____ me, yet will I _____ in him: but I will maintain mine own _____ before him.

3. Proverbs 24:14

So shall the knowledge of _____ be unto thy _____: when thou hast found it, then there shall be a reward, and thy _____ shall not be cut off.

4. Proverbs 24:20
For there shall be no reward to the _____ man; the candle of the _____ shall be put out.

5. Romans 8:24–25
For we are saved by _____: but hope that is seen is not _____: for what a man seeth, why doth he yet hope for? But if we hope for that we see not, then do we with _____ wait for it.

6. 1 Corinthians 15:19
If in this _____ only we have hope in _____, we are of all men most _____.

7. Hebrews 11:1
Now _____ is the substance of things _____ for, the evidence of _____ not seen.

8. 1 Peter 1:3
Blessed be the _____ and Father of our Lord Jesus _____, which according to his abundant mercy hath begotten us again unto a lively hope by the _____ of Jesus Christ from the _____.

51 Scriptures on Love

1. Leviticus 19:17–18
Thou shalt not hate thy _____ in thine heart: thou shalt in any wise rebuke thy neighbour, and not suffer _____ upon him. Thou shalt not avenge, nor bear any grudge against the _____ of thy people, but thou shalt _____ thy neighbour as thyself: I am the LORD.

2. Psalm 30:5

For his _____ endureth but a moment; in his favour is _____: weeping may endure for a _____, but joy cometh in the morning.

3. Psalm 103:8

The _____ is merciful and _____, slow to anger, and plenteous in _____.

4. Psalm 103:13

Like as a _____ pitieth his _____, so the LORD pitieth them that fear _____.

5. Psalm 143:8

Cause me to hear thy lovingkindness in the _____; for in thee do I trust: cause me to know the way wherein I should _____; for I lift up my soul unto thee.

6. Proverbs 10:12

_____ stirreth up strifes: but _____ covereth all sins.

7. Proverbs 21:21

He that followeth after _____ and mercy findeth _____, righteousness, and honour.

8. Isaiah 43:4

Since thou wast precious in my _____, thou hast been honourable, and I have loved _____: therefore will I give _____ for thee, and people for thy _____.

9. Matthew 5:44

But I say unto you, _____ your _____, bless them that curse you, do good to them that hate you, and pray for them which despitefully use you, and persecute _____.

10. Mark 12:30

And thou shalt _____ the Lord thy God with all thy _____, and with all thy soul, and with all thy mind, and with all thy strength: this is the first _____.

11. Mark 12:31

And the second is like, namely this, Thou shalt
_____ thy neighbour as thyself. There is none
other _____ greater than these.

12. Luke 10:27

And he answering said, _____ shalt love the
Lord thy God with all thy _____, and with all thy
_____, and with all thy strength, and with all thy
mind; and thy neighbour as thyself.

13. John 14:21

He that hath my _____, and keepeth them, he it
is that _____ me: and he that loveth me shall be
loved of my _____, and I will love him, and will
manifest myself to him.

14. John 15:12

This is my _____, That ye _____ one another, as I have _____ you.

15. John 15:13

Greater love hath no _____ than this, that a man
lay down his _____ for his _____.

16. Romans 8:38–39

For I am _____, that neither death, nor life, nor angels, nor principalities, nor _____, nor things present, nor things to come, Nor _____, nor depth,
nor any other creature, shall be able to separate us from the
love of _____, which is in Christ Jesus our Lord.

17. Romans 12:9

Let _____ be without dissimulation. Abhor that
which is _____; cleave to that which is good.

18. Romans 12:10

Be kindly affectioned one to another with brotherly
_____; in honour preferring one another.

19. Romans 13:8

Owe no man any thing, but to _____ one another:
for he that loveth another hath fulfilled the _____.

20. Romans 13:10

_____ worketh no _____ to his neigh-
bour: therefore love is the fulfilling of the law.

21. 1 Corinthians 2:9

But as it is _____, Eye hath not seen, nor ear
_____, neither have entered into the heart of
man, the things which God hath prepared for them that
_____ him.

22. 1 Corinthians 10:24

Let no _____ seek his own, but every man another's _____.

23. 1 Corinthians 13:1

Though I speak with the _____ of men and of
_____, and have not charity, I am become as
sounding brass, or a tinkling _____.

24. 1 Corinthians 13:2

And though I have the gift of _____, and under-
stand all _____, and all knowledge; and though I
have all faith, so that I could remove _____, and
have not charity, I am nothing.

25. 1 Corinthians 13:3

And though I bestow all my _____ to feed the
poor, and though I give my _____ to be burned,
and have not charity, it profiteth me _____.

26. 1 Corinthians 13:4–5

_____ suffereth long, and is kind; charity envieth
not; charity vaunteth not itself, is not puffed up, doth not
_____ itself unseemly, seeketh not her own, is not
easily provoked, thinketh no _____.

27. 1 Corinthians 16:14

Let all your _____ be done with _____.

28. Ephesians 3:16–17

That he would grant you, according to the _____ of his _____, to be strengthened with might by his _____ in the inner man; that Christ may dwell in your hearts by faith; that ye, being rooted and grounded in _____.

29. Ephesians 4:2

With all lowliness and _____, with longsuffering, forbearing one another in _____.

30. Ephesians 4:15

But speaking the truth in _____, may grow up into him in all _____, which is the head, even _____.

31. Ephesians 5:2

And walk in love, as Christ also hath _____ us, and hath given _____ for us an offering and a sacrifice to _____ for a sweetsmelling savour.

32. Ephesians 5:25–26

_____, love your _____, even as Christ also loved the church, and gave himself for it; That he might sanctify and cleanse it with the washing of water by the word.

33. Colossians 3:14

And above all these things put on _____, which is the bond of _____.

34. 1 Thessalonians 3:12

And the Lord make you to increase and abound in _____ one toward another, and toward all _____, even as we do toward you.

35. 2 Thessalonians 3:5

And the Lord direct your _____ into the love of God, and into the _____ waiting for Christ.

36. 2 Timothy 1:7

For God hath not given us the spirit of _____; but of power, and of love, and of a sound _____.

37. 1 Peter 4:8

And above all things have fervent _____ among yourselves: for charity shall cover the multitude of

_____.

38. 1 John 3:1

Behold, what manner of love the _____ hath bestowed upon _____, that we should be called the sons of God: therefore the world knoweth us not, because it knew him not.

39. 1 John 3:11

For this is the message that ye heard from the _____, that we should _____ one another.

40. 1 John 4:9

In this was manifested the _____ of God toward us, because that God sent his only begotten Son into the _____, that we might live through him.

41. 1 John 4:10

Herein is _____, not that we loved God, but that he loved us, and sent his _____ to be the propitiation for our _____.

42. 1 John 4:12

No man hath seen _____ at any time. If we love one another, God dwelleth in us, and his love is perfected in

_____.

43. 1 John 4:16

And we have known and believed the _____ that God hath to us. God is _____; and he that dwelleth in love dwelleth in God, and God in him.

44. 1 John 4:18

There is no fear in love; but perfect _____ casteth out _____: because fear hath torment. He that feareth is not made perfect in _____.

45. 1 John 4:20

If a man say, I love God, and hateth his brother, he is a _____: for he that loveth not his _____ whom he hath seen, how can he love God whom he hath not seen?

46. Revelation 3:19

As many as I _____, I rebuke and _____: be zealous therefore, and repent.

52 Crossword Puzzle 1

Tackle this first of three crossword puzzles for 25 bonus points. Since crossword puzzles are difficult by nature, you are allowed three mistakes without penalty.

Across

2. Caspar, Balthazar, and Melchior
4. Christian symbol
6. First gardener
7. Apostle to the Gentiles
8. Proverbs 19:15, Slothfulness casteth into a deep sleep; and an ___ soul shall suffer hunger
11. Chief heavenly messenger, like Gabriel
13. Daniel 7:1, In the first year of Belshazzar king of Babylon Daniel had a dream and visions of his head upon his ___
14. A gift to the infant Jesus
17. Certain man of the cloth
18. Psalm 106:16, They envied Moses also in the camp, and Aaron the ___ of the LORD
19. Adore to the fullest
22. Genesis 7:22, ___ whose nostrils was the breath of life, of all that was in the dry land, died (2 words)
23. Confidence that God's Word is true
25. Period beginning Ash Wednesday
26. Church building feature
27. Mother of Abel
28. The wages of it are death

Down

1. How great thou ___
2. Proverbs 7:17, I have perfumed my bed with ___, aloes, and cinnamon
3. Nazareth's locale
5. Revelation 8:11, And the name of the ___ is called Wormwood
7. He ordered Christ's crucifixion
9. The Ten Commandments, for example
10. Man originally called Simon
12. Thing with verses in the Bible
14. What God has given so that people can make their own choices (2 words)
15. Christmas scene
16. Twin in Genesis
17. Kind of story Jesus told
20. Genesis 11:1, And the whole earth was of ___ language
21. The enemy to us all
23. Genesis 19:24, Then the LORD rained upon Sodom and upon Gomorrah brimstone and ___
24. Psalm 9:17, The wicked shall be turned into ___, and all the nations that forget God

SECTION 2

THE INTERMEDIATE SECTION

This section gets into very specific and challenging questions and puzzles geared to take you to an extreme level of Bible brilliance. (Answers to section 2 begin on page 237.)

> If we abide by the principles taught in the Bible, our country will go on prospering but if we and our posterity neglect its instructions and authority, no man can tell how sudden a catastrophe may overwhelm us and bury all our glory in profound obscurity.
>
> Daniel Webster, American statesman and the fourteenth US secretary of state

53 | Did You Know? (Set 7)

Here is the seventh set of astounding biblical facts.

- Sheep are the animals mentioned most often in the Bible.
- A man named Ben-Hur (son of Hur) was once an officer over Israel (1 Kings 4:7–8 NKJV).
- In his day, Moses was the most humble man on the face of the earth (Numbers 12:3).
- Zechariah 6:14 mentions a man named Hen.
- The king of Babylon tried to foretell the future by examining liver (Ezekiel 21:21).
- When the angel of the Lord delivered a pestilence upon the land of Israel, he could actually be seen in the sky holding a sword in his hand (2 Samuel 24:15–17; 1 Chronicles 21:14–17).
- King Solomon built God's temple in seven years but took thirteen years to build his own palace (1 Kings 6:38; 7:1).

Specialized True or False Trivia

For 1 point per correct answer, tackle this section of true or false statements derived from all areas of the Bible. Some are easy, and some are quite difficult. Do one group at a time and record your score.

Remember, you may do a single group as many times as necessary before posting your best score. It is far more important to be thorough and to learn this information than to finish quickly and retain little.

54 Group 1

1. _____ Isaac was the son of Abraham.

2. _____ Matthew was David's firstborn son.

3. _____ Solomon's son Shaphat became king after him.

4. _____ The apostle Paul said that a woman's long hair is her pride and joy.

5. _____ Flesh and blood is unable to inherit the kingdom of God.

6. _____ In the Bible, sin is called the sting of death.

7. _____ All believers are called to be the temple of God, according to Paul.

8. _____ Paul refers to himself as a missionary in the book of 1 Corinthians.

9. _____ David promised Bathsheba that her son Solomon would one day be governor.

10. _____ Rehoboam ruled in Judah for twenty-one years.

11. _____ King Ahab was the husband of Jezebel.

12. _____ In Samaria, Ahab built a temple for Baal.

13. _____ Elisha brought a widow's son back from the dead in Zarephath.

14. _____ Ravens brought Elijah food in a dire situation.

15. _____ On Mount Nebo, Elijah met the prophets of Baal.

16. _____ Elijah once outran a king's chariot to the town of Jezreel.

17. _____ The prophet Elijah was fed three meals by an angel.

18. _____ When Elijah fled from Jezebel, he went to Mount Horeb.

19. _____ Mount Horeb is called the mount of God.

20. _____ King Solomon had twelve thousand horsemen.

55 Group 2

1. _____ Abner was the commander of Solomon's army.

2. _____ David received permission from the Lord to build the temple.

3. _____ In Solomon's first year as king, he began to build the house of the Lord.

4. _____ Jesus is the chief cornerstone.

5. _____ The apostle Peter compared the devil to a roaring lion.

6. _____ Hannah received a son after asking God to bless her with a child.

7. _____ The first king of Israel was Saul.

8. _____ A person's hand was the part of the body that was usually anointed.

9. _____ Because King Saul acted as a priest in Samuel's place, he was rejected.

10. _____ David's father was Jesse.

11. _____ David had a skill for playing the harp.

12. _____ David boasted of killing a pig and a horse.

13. _____ Bartimaeus was healed of blindness.

14. _____ The gigantic Goliath was from the city of Ekron.

15. _____ Goliath stood over nine feet tall (six cubits and a span).

16. _____ David took seven stones from the brook before killing Goliath.

17. _____ To bring down Goliath, David used a huge sword.

18. _____ David stored Goliath's armor in his tent.

19. _____ Saul once threw a javelin at David.

20. _____ David's first wife was Michal.

56 Group 3

1. _____ The women of Israel danced when Goliath was killed by David.

2. _____ Hannah made a robe every year for her son.

3. _____ In 1 Samuel, Jonathan and David made a covenant of friendship.

4. _____ The priest of Nod gave Saul's sword to David.

5. _____ Saul massacred eighty-five priests in the town of Nazareth.

6. _____ David's wife Abigail was also married to a man named Nabal.

7. _____ At night Saul visited a medium.

8. _____ When Samuel was a boy, he was awakened out of his sleep by the voice of God.

9. _____ Saul's bones were buried under a bridge at Jabesh.

10. _____ Saul's sons were killed by the Philistines.

11. _____ King Saul was critically wounded by Philistine arrows.

12. _____ Six of Saul's sons were killed in battle.

13. _____ Eli's sons were killed when the ark was taken.

14. _____ The ark of the covenant was taken into battle with the Philistines by Eli's sons.

15. _____ Dagon was the god of the Philistines.

16. _____ Samuel, a judge and a prophet, built an altar to the Lord at Ramah.

17. _____ Samuel's home was in the city of Ramah.

18. _____ Kish was the father of King Saul.

19. _____ Jesus Christ is the mediator between God and man.

20. _____ Paul told Timothy that Christians should lift up a symbol of the cross in prayer.

57 Group 4

1. _____ Abijah, the king of Judah, had fourteen wives.

2. _____ The Philistines brought a tribute to King Jehoshaphat.

3. _____ In a vision, the prophet Micaiah saw the Lord sitting upon a mountain.

4. _____ Solomon got the cedars for his temple from Lebanon.

5. _____ King Uzziah dug wells in the desert.

6. _____ Uzziah, the king of Judah, was a leper until he died.

7. _____ Moses disguised himself before fighting with an Egyptian.

8. _____ Paul's nationality was Greek.

9. _____ Paul suffered shipwrecks three times.

10. _____ Eve's name appears seven times in the New Testament.

11. _____ The apostle Paul fled from the soldiers of King Aretas in Damascus.

12. _____ Paul knew of a man who had been caught up into the third heaven.

13. _____ The bones of Elisha healed a man of leprosy.

14. _____ Elijah was taken to heaven in a whirlwind.

15. _____ When Elisha struck the Jordan River with Elijah's cloak, it turned red.

16. _____ Elisha was used by God to heal the waters of Gibeah with a bowl of salt.

17. _____ Hezekiah and Joshua had time altered for them.

18. _____ Josiah was only eight years old when he became king, and he reigned in Jerusalem thirty-one years.

19. _____ King Josiah was killed in Megiddo.

20. _____ Nebuchadnezzar was a ruler of Babylon.

58 Group 5

1. _____ David was the last king of Judah.

2. _____ Elisha's servant was Gehazi.

3. _____ Elisha supplied a widow with large quantities of milk and honey.

4. _____ For lying to the prophet Elisha, Gehazi was turned into a leper.

5. _____ Elisha's servant had a vision of the hills filled with horses and chariots of fire.

6. _____ Hazael murdered King Benhadad.

7. _____ The prophet Urijah was murdered for opposing King Jehoiakim.

8. _____ King Jehu ordered Jezebel's servants to toss her out the window.

9. _____ After Jezebel's death, wild horses ate her body.

10. _____ David saw his neighbor bathing on a rooftop.

11. _____ Nathan, a prophet, confronted King David about his sin of adultery.

12. _____ Absalom was David and Bathsheba's second son.

13. _____ God named Solomon Jedidiah.

14. _____ After killing his brother Amnon, Absalom fled to Geshur for three years.

15. _____ David's son Absalom was known for being an unattractive man.

16. _____ As David went up the Mount of Olives, he was barefoot and wept.

17. _____ Absalom was buried by Joab in a great pit in the forest.

18. _____ David was anointed king at Hebron.

19. _____ Saul's son Ishbosheth was made king over Israel by Abner.

20. _____ King Saul's son Ishbosheth was also known as Titus.

59 Group 6

1. _____ The wise woman of Abel saved her city by negotiating with Joab.

2. _____ Joab killed a man while kissing him.

3. _____ David moved the bones of Saul and his son Jonathan to their final place of burial.

4. _____ Saul's grandson Mephibosheth was crippled in both feet.

5. _____ While pretending to get wheat, Rechab and Baanah killed a king.

6. _____ Amorites inhabited Jerusalem before the Israelites.

7. _____ In her heart, Michal despised her husband, David.

8. _____ Jehu was the commander of David's army.

9. _____ Timothy's grandmother's name was Hilda.

10. _____ Lydia was Timothy's mother.

11. _____ Paul sent Tychicus to Ephesus.

12. _____ Four soldiers were stationed with Peter in his cell.

13. _____ Matthias succeeded Judas Iscariot as an apostle.

14. _____ Peter led a Roman soldier named Cornelius to Christ.

15. _____ Cornelius was baptized by Peter.

16. _____ Believers were first called Christians at the church in Thessalonica.

17. _____ Agabus prophesied there would be a famine in the land.

18. _____ Philip was the first apostle to be martyred.

19. _____ The first apostle to be martyred was James.

20. _____ Herod ordered the jail keepers be put to death after Peter escaped.

60 Group 7

1. _____ Herod was eaten by worms before he died.
2. _____ Peter was released from prison by an angel.
3. _____ Barnabas and Paul were deserted by Mark in Perga.
4. _____ The apostle Paul was originally known as Saul.
5. _____ Paul was stoned in the city of Lystra.
6. _____ Silas, Paul's traveling companion, was considered a prophet.
7. _____ On Paul's second missionary journey, he was accompanied by John the Baptist.
8. _____ Lydia was a seller of purple cloth.
9. _____ The Lord opened Lydia's heart to respond to Paul's message.
10. _____ Lydia was baptized by Paul and Silas.
11. _____ The Bereans were famous for writing gospel songs.
12. _____ Claudius demanded all the Jews depart from Rome.
13. _____ Crispus, a synagogue leader, was a member of the church in Corinth.
14. _____ The church in Ephesus was the scene of a burning of wicked books.
15. _____ The school of Tyrannus was in Corinth.
16. _____ John preached at Pentecost.
17. _____ Eutychus was in Assos when he fell out of a window.
18. _____ Both Paul and Peter raised people from the dead.
19. _____ Paul's hometown was Tarsus in Cilicia.
20. _____ Paul's teacher was a famous rabbi named Gamaliel.

61 Group 8

1. _____ Paul studied under Gamaliel.

2. _____ Paul's nephew came to sing Paul songs while he was imprisoned in Jerusalem.

3. _____ Forty men made an oath to fast until they had killed Paul.

4. _____ Tertullus prosecuted Paul when he was in Caesarea.

5. _____ Festus replaced Felix as governor of Judea.

6. _____ Felix, wanting to do a favor for the Jews, let Paul out of prison.

7. _____ Euroclydon was the name of a false god.

8. _____ Paul was not affected when a viper bit him.

9. _____ James healed a crippled man at the Beautiful Gate.

10. _____ Barnabas means "the son of consolation."

11. _____ Barnabas means "the son of peace."

12. _____ Bartholomew was Barnabas's original name.

13. _____ About six thousand men accepted Christ when Peter spoke on the day of Pentecost.

14. _____ A Pharisee was considered a servant.

15. _____ Gamaliel was described as a teacher of the law.

16. _____ Stephen was the first Christian to be martyred.

17. _____ Stephen was stoned to death.

18. _____ An angel carried Philip from Gaza to Azotus.

19. _____ King David tried to buy the gifts of the Holy Spirit.

20. _____ Peter was headed to Damascus to arrest Christians.

62 Group 9

1. _____ Aeneas was healed from palsy by John the Baptist.

2. _____ John the Baptist raised Dorcas from the dead.

3. _____ After the apostle Paul saw a vision of Jesus, he temporarily lost his sight.

4. _____ Before Amos was a prophet, he was a carpenter.

5. _____ Amos spoke about justice rolling down like a boulder.

6. _____ Paul told believers to set their affections on things around them.

7. _____ Paul described his friend Luke as a beloved brother.

8. _____ Nebuchadnezzar was king of Egypt.

9. _____ Before the Babylonians changed Meshach's Jewish name, it was Daniel.

10. _____ Nebuchadnezzar had worrisome dreams that kept him from sleeping.

11. _____ Nebuchadnezzar promised various gifts, rewards, and great honor to the person who could interpret his dream.

12. _____ During Belshazzar's feast, a mysterious hand wrote on the wall.

13. _____ David was the only king in the Bible referred to as "the Mede."

14. _____ King Darius ordered Daniel be thrown into the lions' den.

15. _____ Daniel would kneel and pray five times a day.

16. _____ King Darius fasted after Daniel was thrown into the lions' den.

17. _____ Daniel had a vision of a horse with eagle's wings.

18. _____ The angel Gabriel gave Daniel an understanding of the future.

19. _____ The angel Gabriel visited David while he was confessing his sins.

20. _____ When Moses died, he was 130 years old.

63 Group 10

1. _____ Eleazar succeeded his father, Aaron, as priest.

2. _____ The Israelites were commanded to bring firstborn animals to God for sacrifice.

3. _____ Og, the king of Bashan, had a bed made of iron.

4. _____ On the mountain of Nebo, Moses was given a view into the Promised Land.

5. _____ During the time of Moses, the city of Jericho was also known as the city of palm trees.

6. _____ God buried Moses in the land of Moab.

7. _____ The Israelites mourned Moses for seventy days.

8. _____ The Lord tells us to honor our mother and father.

9. _____ God described the Israelites as being stiffnecked.

10. _____ The book of Ecclesiastes says laughter is madness (NKJV).

11. _____ In Ephesians, sleepers are told to rise from the dead.

12. _____ Paul recommended the Holy Spirit as a substitute for food.

13. _____ Adah was Esther's Hebrew name.

14. _____ Esther was an orphan.

15. _____ Haman was angry with Mordecai because he stole his cattle.

16. _____ Haman planned to destroy all the Jews.

17. _____ Tamar was the wife of Haman of Persia.

18. _____ The Egyptians made the Israelites into slaves.

19. _____ Pharaoh made a false confession to Moses and Aaron.

20. _____ God blew a strong west wind and stopped the locust plague.

Word Searches

64 Names of God Part 1

Find the Bible words for God in this puzzle. If you find all the words, give yourself 10 points.

```
Q U E M U N M G R E A T I A M
H H S G N I K F O G N I K Y K
G A W R C B H Y U C L A V G D
V I N N E T S G X U R H Y A Z
H S H W P T D O G F O B M A L
Y S R O I V A S H L A L P H A
A E F V A N F W Y L K J S T Z
S M T E S C S S G K C Y Q S P
H Y V H A E P A C N E M B I G
E Q K Y E I J O U O I I F R R
W V Q M R V R Y E M V V V H E
A Q Z I G E I K V E D Y I C H
T B T H H N Q N P G J G D L G
A B M T G D S F E A T A T O D
G O O D S H E P H E R D D T R
```

ALPHA	KING OF KINGS	SAVIOR
CHRIST	LAMB OF GOD	THE ROCK
GOOD SHEPHERD	LIVING WATER	THE VINE
GREAT I AM	MESSIAH	YASHEWA
HOLY SPIRIT	OMEGA	

65 Names of God Part 2

Here are the same names of God but in a different puzzle. If you find all the words, give yourself 10 points.

```
P M R O I V A S F K N H J D L
U H E F B R H T R K J R F N F
S F D S T I R I P S Y L O H D
U G O I S Q O O F K I F A Y R
O B N J Z I J W H C I J Y A E
L W V I Y L A J L O P V N S T
A K K H K K L H C R H P O H A
M K Z V P F T A M E L J E E W
B Q G V L S O A M H N V L W G
O U G X I F I G O T I T E A N
F R Y R O T T S N N S Y U W I
G T H M A S H N E I B Z E C V
O C E E J I F I U A K U H X I
D G R A H P L A F V W W H D L
A G O O D S H E P H E R D F A
```

ALPHA	KING OF KINGS	SAVIOR
CHRIST	LAMB OF GOD	THE ROCK
GOOD SHEPHERD	LIVING WATER	THE VINE
GREAT I AM	MESSIAH	YASHEWA
HOLY SPIRIT	OMEGA	

66 Names of God Part 3

Try to find the same fourteen names for God as you did in the previous two word searches, but this time you do not have the word list. If you are successful, give yourself 25 points.

```
L I V I N G W A T E R O N N J
G O O D S H E P H E R D K D Z
A Z I X V P I V N E R A L T Z
H G J E F J K W F U H U I W E
P F Q N S A V I O R K R U C H
L J S I J M A M Y K I T H M S
A W D V P B E I B P N A Z A S
M Z E E D G N D S V G G M G G
B A D H A K W Y K C O R E H T
O D W T U B L E I C F E S R P
F W G E L O M F H X K A S B Z
G Q O B H I L R U X I T I W W
O H X J X S I W T V N I A H A
D K I F X S A G U K G A H W H
D G Y K T D B Y J E S M K P Y
```

67 Abraham's Progeny Part 1

Find the following names of Abraham's progeny. Give yourself 10 points if you find them all.

```
K Z M I D I A N C T C P N L L
E S I A L E U M M I M V Y H N
D H F M F K S M Q M C O W A I
A N D S R U M O E I D V D M Z
R A S H U A H J A Z B E R O G
O S C F F N N V D Z D A B L U
R S Q G D W Z M U A C E W W H
O H E Z R O N P D H W D W C K
P U E P H R A I M J P I O S Y
B R N A Q G O Y J W H N O H J
R I Z B Y A O W V W A W S A G
R M N E B A J O T H R D H M A
G H E I S H M A E L E R E M T
N A H A T H B H T C Z H B A B
J O K S H A N J S H E L A H R
```

ASSHURIM (Genesis 25:3)   JOKSHAN (Genesis 25:2)   PHAREZ (Genesis 38:29)
CARMI (Genesis 46:9)   KEDAR (Genesis 25:13)   SHAMMAH (Genesis 36:13)
DEDAN (Genesis 10:7)   LEUMMIM (Genesis 25:3)   SHEBA (Genesis 10:7)
EPHRAIM (Genesis 41:52)   MIDIAN (Genesis 25:2)   SHELAH (Genesis 38:5)
HANOCH (Genesis 25:4)   MIZZAH (Genesis 36:13)   SHUAH (Genesis 25:2)
HEZRON (Genesis 46:9)   NAHATH (Genesis 36:13)   ZIMRAN (Genesis 25:2)
ISHMAEL (Genesis 16:11)   NEBAJOTH (Genesis 25:13)

68 Abraham's Progeny Part 2

Once again, find the following names. Give yourself 10 points if you find them all.

```
A S S H U R I M U C K X R G D
R S D K H M I Z Z A H H U S L
U K V N V S H U A H K A E Y L
P H A R E Z P E W T K N I Y V
G K L T T I C I V O N O G R E
T H Y S H E B A H A A C A K P
J O K S H A N Y I N A H A T H
S H A M M A H D O C H W D R R
I Q Q F Y Z I M R A N E H A A
B X C H Q M J M L N S W D N I
D O K V C S V E Z W R E M J M
E A Y Z S A H E B J K X I E Q
D K O A W S R K L E U M M I M
A K O V H N F M F H E Z R O N
N E B A J O T H I S H M A E L
```

ASSHURIM	JOKSHAN	PHAREZ
CARMI	KEDAR	SHAMMAH
DEDAN	LEUMMIM	SHEBA
EPHRAIM	MIDIAN	SHELAH
HANOCH	MIZZAH	SHUAH
HEZRON	NAHATH	ZIMRAN
ISHMAEL	NEBAJOTH	

69 Abraham's Progeny Part 3

Give yourself 25 points if you find all twenty names.

```
Q B P K V M B N G J Z Z C N T
Q Z H N W V A L D J Z L J A K
X I A I V D W I E J I Z V Y Z
N M R U E A S S H U R I M Y F
T R E D K T X H D C M X F R S
C A Z T S H A M M A H M A Y H
S N B L K I H A I A S D I P E
H R E G M H S E U Z E U H M L
E V F R T K T L Z K Z C M J A
B E A A E H R N C R O A H O H
A C H A M I D I A N O P H K G
B A N P A G T T A C X N M S M
N E B A J O T H G Q O I Z H C
R Z R Y K E P H R A I M K A R
S H U A H J K E M X O N T N V
```

70 Women in the Bible Part 1

Find the following names of women in the Bible. Give yourself 10 points if you find them all.

```
R X D I N A H E B E O H P H Q
E H A N N A H I N O A M L M B
H N B S F R M L A P L V H D R
T Q R S M I U D E B O R A H O
S I E P A D B T E B I L H A H
E J H V N R V V H O E L J T Y
Q B T K P S A C R O D Z L J R
H A E Q Q N Y H C Q B E E H J
A T B L Z R A B I G A I L J U
L H A G A R G V E H N Q H K D
I S S M Q A G P K E V L U B I
L H I G X C D A M A R I S S T
E E L H Z H Q L P D Q D K T H
D B E A Q E B R A Y H E I F X
C A R O Q L I B M O T X X C O
```

ABIGAIL (1 Samuel 25:3)
AHINOAM (1 Samuel 14:50)
BATHSHEBA (2 Samuel 12:24)
BILHAH (Genesis 29:29)
DAMARIS (Acts 17:34)
DEBORAH (Genesis 35:8)
DELILAH (Judges 16:4)
DINAH (Genesis 30:21)
DORCAS (Acts 9:36)
ELISABETH (Luke 1:7)
ESTHER (book of Esther)
HAGAR (Genesis 16:1)
HANNAH (1 Samuel 1:2)
JEZEBEL (1 Kings 16:31)
JUDITH (Genesis 26:34)
LEAH (Genesis 29:16)
MARY (Matthew 1:16)
PHOEBE (Romans 16:1 NKJV)
RACHEL (Genesis 29:6)
RUTH (book of Ruth)
SARAH (Genesis 17:15)

71 Women in the Bible Part 2

Once again, find the following women's names. If you find them all, give yourself 10 points.

K	E	A	J	H	A	N	I	D	T	J	V	Y	X	C
U	B	M	W	O	K	J	W	H	T	I	D	U	J	J
M	E	F	A	X	L	E	H	C	A	R	A	G	A	H
H	O	E	L	I	S	A	B	E	T	H	Q	I	Y	W
A	H	W	Z	I	H	B	L	J	E	Z	E	B	E	L
N	P	X	A	U	A	Z	F	L	Y	S	N	H	A	E
N	O	C	B	J	H	G	U	F	Z	U	A	S	S	Y
A	R	G	E	S	L	J	I	P	D	R	I	R	M	T
H	E	D	H	A	I	T	O	B	O	R	U	U	A	Q
I	H	E	S	C	B	E	B	B	A	T	R	X	P	H
N	T	L	H	R	Y	G	E	M	H	H	A	E	L	G
O	S	I	T	O	U	D	A	X	M	O	N	I	W	Z
A	E	L	A	D	T	D	D	V	A	Y	U	X	K	A
M	C	A	B	S	P	X	U	B	R	Z	B	F	R	L
P	T	H	T	G	E	M	C	J	Y	X	S	U	N	Z

ABIGAIL	DINAH	JUDITH
AHINOAM	DORCAS	LEAH
BATHSHEBA	ELISABETH	MARY
BILHAH	ESTHER	PHOEBE
DAMARIS	HAGAR	RACHEL
DEBORAH	HANNAH	RUTH
DELILAH	JEZEBEL	SARAH

72 Women in the Bible Part 3

If you find all twenty-one names, give yourself 25 points.

```
N S E U V M A O N I H A L H Q
D E B O R A H K F A M I F Q P
D M E I H Y D U N D A T D R N
Q N O P U O H N H G O J T B M
H Z H I E G A K I H G R R Y I
R B P J I H G B K A E Y C M B
A I X Z E D A A U L S G R A B
C L A H C Z R C I I T O W G S
H H P N A U E S B L H E N Z A
E A D Q U N A B C E E O H F H
L H E G L B I O E D R A C J T
R O B L E D P D P L R Z X M I
U B A T H S H E B A W K A X D
T O H V A X R Q S X C R U X U
H W N S I R A M A D Y X H U J
```

73 Prisoners and Exiles Part 1

Find the following names of prisoners and exiles. If you find them all, give yourself 10 points.

```
S U S M L I S A I A H D O Q P
D I U V O M A N A S S E H M E
J A U U F R Z E D E K I A H T
G O N T M S D O W V Q N D Y E
I X H I R O H E Q T S B O C R
Y K M N E P R S C R Z E Y A S
J W D Q E L J T O A C A I N H
E S Z S F O T H L Q I Z E F G
R X O Q X A X E K L Q A O E N
E J M J Q Z P R J A C O B E X
M Y Z K D A Q A Z L W Z H S R
I U W Z Q R A R U K O P C I X
A L F E G I M D J L E Z A L A
H H M M V A R Y N T H A G A R
Y C T H C H N Z S W X L M S Z
```

AZARIAH (2 Chronicles 26:20)
CAIN (Genesis 4:16)
DANIEL (Daniel 2:20)
ESTHER (book of Esther)
HAGAR (Genesis 21:17)
ISAIAH (2 Kings 19:5)

JACOB (Genesis 28:5)
JEREMIAH (book of Jeremiah)
JOHN (book of John)
JOSEPH (Genesis 37:28)
MANASSEH (Genesis 46:20)
MORDECAI (Esther 7:10)

NOAH (Genesis 8:1)
PAUL (Acts 16:16)
PETER (John 18:27)
SILAS (Acts 15:22)
STEPHEN (Acts 6:5)
ZEDEKIAH (2 Kings 24:20)

74 Prisoners and Exiles Part 2

Once again, give yourself 10 points if you find the following names.

```
Z U K X S Q K X S A C U M N C
E L C Z N B A H T X F X I P V
D A N I E L A S E T K A O V S
E L B J A I V I P S C T R X J
K E X X R S H L H H T J P X Q
I U U A A A J A E W B H P T L
A P Z I I E P S N O J O E U N
H A H A G A R R C J B F A R M
G C S A K R H A Q O G P T P O
O I H W S P J P D H L F S A R
T U X H E Y K O E N S W I V D
V Z A S H F G V Y T D P S C E
V O O G E Q G Y U X E M T G C
N J W M A N A S S E H R M K A
V H X C J E R E M I A H G A I
```

AZARIAH	JACOB	NOAH
CAIN	JEREMIAH	PAUL
DANIEL	JOHN	PETER
ESTHER	JOSEPH	SILAS
HAGAR	MANASSEH	STEPHEN
ISAIAH	MORDECAI	ZEDEKIAH

75 | Prisoners and Exiles Part 3

If you find all eighteen names, give yourself 25 points.

```
D J I I S A I A H T N H J B U
O U W K X T E C A P N A R R B
Z C N C R S E H W Z P G Q G I
N O A H A B A P G W Q A M I X
Z O B L R I K H H J T R U T R
Q E I M R Q A D J E E C Q L R
J S D A A I L G P E N P P E D
N A Z E M N J S F P R C T T A
W A C E K A A D Y L Y E H R N
E D R O X I F S C Y P G A W I
Q E P F B K A B S F E D G S E
J F B V X M L H V E J O H N L
O A J M I X U R X E H N E B D
C A I N P I M O R D E C A I W
J O S E P H E S T H E R I M F
```

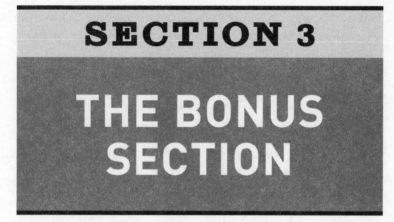

SECTION 3

THE BONUS SECTION

Test your knowledge with these entertaining puzzles. (Answers to section 3 begin on page 247.)

> The nearer I approach to the end of my pilgrimage, the clearer is the evidence of the divine origin of the Bible, and the grandeur and sublimity of God's remedy for fallen man are more appreciated, and the future is illumined with hope and joy.
>
> Francis Bacon, English philosopher, scientist, lawyer, and father of the scientific method

76 Food by the Book

In this admittedly difficult exercise fit for the truly Bible brilliant, give yourself 20 bonus points for each correct answer. This is an open-book exercise. Use of your Bible is permitted.

Dairy Products

1. What dairy product is mentioned in Proverbs 30:33?
2. What dairy product is mentioned in 1 Samuel 17:18; 2 Samuel 17:29; and Job 10:10?
3. What dairy product is mentioned in Isaiah 7:15?
4. What dairy product is mentioned in Job 6:6 and Luke 11:12?
5. What dairy product is mentioned in Exodus 33:3; Judges 5:25; and Job 10:10?

Fruits

1. What fruit is mentioned in Song of Solomon 2:5?
2. What fruit is mentioned in 2 Samuel 6:19 and 1 Chronicles 16:3?
3. What fruit is mentioned in Nehemiah 13:15 and Jeremiah 24:1–3?
4. What fruit is mentioned in Leviticus 19:10 and Deuteronomy 23:24?
5. What fruit is mentioned in Numbers 11:5 and Isaiah 1:8?
6. What fruit is mentioned in Isaiah 17:6 and Micah 6:15?
7. What fruit is mentioned in Numbers 20:5 and Deuteronomy 8:8?
8. What fruit is mentioned in Numbers 6:3 and 2 Samuel 6:19?
9. What fruit is mentioned in Psalm 78:47 and Amos 7:14?

Vegetables

1. What vegetables are mentioned in Numbers 11:5?

2. What vegetables are mentioned in 2 Kings 4:39?

Nuts

1. What nuts are mentioned in Numbers 17:8?

2. What nuts are mentioned in Genesis 43:11?

Legumes

1. What two types of legumes are mentioned in Ezekiel 4:9?

2. What legumes are mentioned in Genesis 25:34 and 2 Samuel 17:28?

Spices and Herbs

1. What three spices or herbs are mentioned in Matthew 23:23?

2. What spice or herb is mentioned in Exodus 16:31 and Numbers 11:7?

3. What spice or herb is mentioned in Exodus 30:23 and Revelation 18:13?

4. What spice or herb is mentioned in both Isaiah 28:25 and Matthew 23:23?

5. What spice or herb is mentioned in Numbers 11:5?

6. What spice or herb is mentioned in both Matthew 23:23 and Luke 11:42?

7. What spice or herb is mentioned in Matthew 13:31?

8. What spice or herb is mentioned in Luke 11:42?

9. What spice or herb is mentioned in Ezra 6:9 and Job 6:6?

Fish

1. Along with fish, how many loaves of bread did Jesus give to his disciples in Matthew 15:36?
2. In John 21:11, who pulled up a net full of 153 fish?

Various Grains

1. What grain is mentioned in Deuteronomy 8:8 and Ezekiel 4:9?
2. What grain is mentioned in Genesis 25:34; 2 Samuel 6:19; 16:1; and Mark 8:14?
3. What grain is mentioned in Matthew 12:1?
4. What grain is mentioned in 2 Samuel 17:28 and 1 Kings 17:12?
5. What grains are mentioned in Ezekiel 4:9?
6. What grain is mentioned in Genesis 19:3 and Exodus 12:20?
7. What grain is mentioned in Deuteronomy 8:8 and Ezra 6:9?

Various Meats

1. What type of meat is mentioned in Proverbs 15:17 and Luke 15:23?
2. What type of meat is mentioned in Genesis 27:9?
3. What type of meat is mentioned in 2 Samuel 12:4?
4. What type of meat is mentioned in 1 Kings 19:21?
5. What type of meat is mentioned in Deuteronomy 14:4?
6. What type of meat is mentioned in Genesis 27:7?

Various Fowl

1. What type of fowl/bird is mentioned in 1 Samuel 26:20 and Jeremiah 17:11?
2. What type of fowl/bird is mentioned in Genesis 15:9 and Leviticus 12:8?
3. What type of fowl/bird is mentioned in Psalm 105:40?
4. What type of fowl/bird is mentioned in Leviticus 12:8?

Miscellaneous

1. What drink, suitable for children or adults, is mentioned in Numbers 6:3 (NIV)?
2. What healthy food is mentioned in Exodus 33:3; Deuteronomy 8:8; and Judges 14:8–9?
3. What type of oil is mentioned in Deuteronomy 8:8 and Ezra 6:9?
4. What type of liquid is mentioned in Ruth 2:14 and John 19:29?
5. What drink is mentioned in Ezra 6:9 and John 2:1–10?

77 Crossword Puzzle 2

This crossword puzzle is supersized. Give yourself 50 bonus points if you solve it with five or fewer mistakes.

Across

7. With what Jesus fed 5,000 (3 words)
11. 1 Kings 16:30, And ___ the son of Omri did evil
12. ___ the Bible every day
14. 1 Samuel 14:14, And that first slaughter, which Jonathan and his armourbearer made, was about twenty men, within as it were an half ___ of land
15. Genesis 1:27, So God created man in his own image, in the image of God created he ___
17. Abraham's grandson
19. Jerusalem's region
20. Exodus 16:28, And the LORD said unto Moses, How long refuse ye to keep my commandments and my ___?
21. Jeremiah 2:32, Can a maid forget her ornaments, or a bride her ___?
23. Atone for something, with "oneself"
25. Event in Luke, with "the"
27. Apostle to the Gentiles
28. Psalm 128:3, Thy wife shall be as a fruitful ___ by the sides of thine house
29. Leviticus 19:5, And if ye offer a sacrifice of peace offerings unto the LORD, ye shall offer ___ your own will (2 words)
31. Adam's mate
33. Genesis 17:5, Neither shall thy name ___ more be called Abram
34. What those who believe in Jesus Christ shall have (2 words)
36. Brother of Moses
37. Opposite of loves
39. First paradise (3 words)
41. A female follower of Jesus during his time on earth (2 words)
46. "The evidence of things not seen" (Hebrews 11:1)
48. Genesis 24:29, And Rebekah ___ brother, and his name was Laban (2 words)
49. ". . . LORD is against them that do ___" (Psalm 34:16)

50. Greed, envy, or pride
51. Exodus 9:9, And it shall become ___ dust in all the land of Egypt
52. 1 John 2:18, Little children, it is the last time: and as ye have heard that ___ shall come
53. 2 Samuel 22:6, The sorrows of ___ compassed me about; the snares of death prevented me

Down

1. Priest's gown
2. Man ___ wife
3. Standard Holy Bible (3 words)
4. Opposite of he
5. Abraham, Isaac, or Jacob
6. December holiday
8. "Jesus wept" in the Bible
9. Matthew 2:2, ". . . for we have seen his ___ in the east"
10. 1 Chronicles 16:30, Fear before him, all the earth: the world also shall be ___, that it be not moved
13. Term referring to the Almighty
16. Jesus's early profession
18. Features of some modern Bibles
22. What Jesus calmed (2 words)
24. Beelzebub
26. See 24-Down
30. Father of James and John
31. God, in Hebrew texts
32. Holiday when the hymn "Rise Again" is sung
35. Third book of the New Testament
38. Prophet who anointed Saul and David as kings
39. What was written on the commandments (2 words)
40. Genesis 16:16, And Abram was fourscore and six years old, when Hagar bare ___ to Abram
42. First human
43. Forty-day period before Easter
44. Member of the family
45. Three came from the East
46. Go without food purposely
47. Genesis 43:21, And it came to pass, when we came to the ___, that we opened our sacks

78 Crossword Puzzle 3

Award yourself 50 bonus points if you complete this puzzle with five or fewer mistakes.

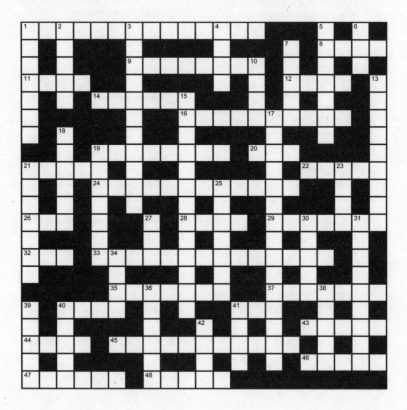

Across

1. Ceremony in which something is made holy
8. Biblical birthright seller
9. Christianity is one
11. Prophet Elisha cursed a bunch of youths for making fun of a ___ man
12. Lazarus was raised from the ___
14. Matthew 10:3, ___, and Bartholomew; Thomas, and Matthew the publican
16. Prayer topic, often
19. A name for Jesus (3 words)
20. Genesis 6:13, And God said unto Noah, The ___ of all flesh is come
21. ". . . the ___ of God was upon him" (Luke 2:40)
22. ___ of Cyrene
24. What Easter celebrates
26. Go against God
28. First gardener
29. Name for Jesus
32. Romans 3:23, For ___ have sinned, and come short of the glory of God
33. Whom we worship (3 words)
35. The devil
37. Human-made rules that can contradict 21-Down (2 words)
40. Apostle to the Gentiles
41. Adam's mate
43. Old Testament books labeled I and II
44. ". . . for we have seen his ___ in the east"
45. Jesus was born via it (2 words)
46. Genesis 12:9, And Abram journeyed, going on ___ toward the south
47. Prophet who anointed Saul and David as kings
48. Salome danced for him

Down

1. Day of rest
2. 2 Chronicles 3:9, And the weight of the ___ was fifty shekels of gold
3. What Jesus recommends one offer to his brothers
4. Matthew 4:4, But he answered and said, ___ written, Man shall not live by bread alone (2 words)
5. Atonement for sins
6. Genesis 1:4, And God ___ the light, that it was good
7. What 48-Across was king of
10. Psalm 55:17, Evening, and morning, and at ___, will I pray, and cry aloud
13. Book before Haggai
15. Belief that each individual human soul existed before conception (2 words)
17. What God gave Moses on Mount Sinai (2 words)
18. Where there will be no more crying
19. Aaron's rod, at one point
21. It is greater than 37-Across (2 words)
23. Three came from the East
25. Part of a Bible book
27. Remains of a burnt offering?
30. See 35-Across
31. Michael or Gabriel
34. Opposite of 18-Down
36. Body of Christians, especially on Sundays?
38. Mark, for one
39. The Christ
40. One of 150 in the Bible
41. ". . . Lord is against them that do ___" (Psalm 34:16)
42. Do ___ others as . . .

ANSWERS

Section 1: The Must-Know Section

1. Do Not Be Fooled

1. False, that phrase does not appear in the Bible at all.
2. False, the Bible does not mention an "apple," only "fruit."
3. False, that phrase is from a seventeenth-century poem by Samuel Butler.
4. False, that phrase is from a poem by English poet William Cowper, who was born in 1731.
5. False, that phrase is not written in any book of the Bible.
6. False, the Bible does not give a specific number of wise men.
7. False, "The Little Drummer Boy" is a Christmas carol and is not based on any biblical character.
8. False, according to Jonah 1:17, Jonah was in the belly of "a great fish."
9. False, the Bible never mentions Satan taking the form of or entering into the serpent in the garden of Eden.
10. False, this phrase does not appear anywhere in the Bible.
11. False, 1 Timothy 6:10 says, "For *the love of* money is the root of all evil."
12. False, "To thine own self be true" was written by Shakespeare in act 1 of *Hamlet*.
13. False, "Love the sinner, hate the sin" does not appear in the Bible. St. Augustine wrote it in a letter in the fifth century AD.
14. False, according to Matthew 2:11, by the time the wise men visited Jesus, he was in a "house."
15. False, there were two sets. Moses broke one set in anger when he saw the false idol, the golden calf (Exodus 32:19; 34:1).

I hope you scored well on your first test. Simply knowing that these fifteen "facts" are all false puts you ahead of the vast majority of the public. You are well on your way to becoming Bible brilliant.

2. The Essentials

1. "In the beginning God created the heaven and the earth" (Genesis 1:1)
2. Mary (Matthew 1:18)
3. Garden of Eden (Genesis 2:8)
4. Serpent (Genesis 3:1–6)
5. Crucifixion (Mark 15:24–25)
6. Death (Romans 6:23)
7. Aaron (Exodus 7:1)
8. Murder (Genesis 4:8)
9. Daniel (Daniel 6:16)
10. God's (Genesis 1:27)
11. "Our Father which art in heaven" (Matthew 6:9)
12. Loaves of bread and fishes (Matthew 14:15–20)
13. Rib (Genesis 2:21–22)
14. Blasphemy against the Holy Ghost (Matthew 12:31; Mark 3:29)
15. Dust (Genesis 2:7)
16. Flood (Genesis 7:7)
17. Peter (Matthew 26:69–74)
18. Crown of thorns (Matthew 27:29)
19. Cain (Genesis 4:9)
20. Stone (Exodus 34:1; Deuteronomy 5:22)
21. Twelve (Luke 6:13)
22. Shepherds (Luke 2:8–17)
23. Exodus
24. Shepherd (1 Samuel 17:12–15)
25. Genesis
26. Matthew
27. He struck him with a stone from his sling (1 Samuel 17:48–50)
28. Judaea (Matthew 3:1)
29. This is Jesus the King of the Jews (Matthew 27:37)
30. Manger (Luke 2:7)
31. Abraham (James 2:21–22)
32. She was a virgin (Matthew 1:22–25)
33. Forty (Genesis 7:12)
34. Moses (Exodus 2:3)
35. He was swallowed by a great fish (Jonah 1:17)
36. She was Naomi's daughter-in-law (Ruth 1:4)
37. Joseph (Matthew 1:18–19)
38. Psalms
39. Swine (Matthew 8:32)
40. Psalm 23 (Psalm 23:1)
41. Paul (Romans 1:1–Jude 1:25)
42. They tossed him into a pit and eventually sold him to strangers (Genesis 37:23–28)
43. Jesse (1 Samuel 17:12; Ruth 4:17, 22)
44. David (Matthew 1:6)
45. Revelation
46. Amen (Revelation 22:21)
47. Sixty-six
48. He washed their feet (John 13:1–5)
49. Cain (Genesis 4:1)
50. Six days (Exodus 20:11)

3. Books of the Bible

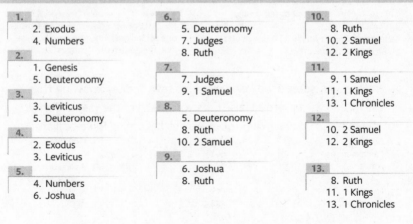

1.
2. Exodus
4. Numbers

2.
1. Genesis
5. Deuteronomy

3.
3. Leviticus
5. Deuteronomy

4.
2. Exodus
3. Leviticus

5.
4. Numbers
6. Joshua

6.
5. Deuteronomy
7. Judges
8. Ruth

7.
7. Judges
9. 1 Samuel

8.
5. Deuteronomy
8. Ruth
10. 2 Samuel

9.
6. Joshua
8. Ruth

10.
8. Ruth
10. 2 Samuel
12. 2 Kings

11.
9. 1 Samuel
11. 1 Kings
13. 1 Chronicles

12.
10. 2 Samuel
12. 2 Kings

13.
8. Ruth
11. 1 Kings
13. 1 Chronicles

14.
12. 2 Kings
15. Ezra
18. Job

15.
15. Ezra
17. Esther
19. Psalms

16.
16. Nehemiah
20. Proverbs

17.
15. Ezra
18. Job
20. Proverbs

18.
12. 2 Kings
15. Ezra
17. Esther
20. Proverbs

19.
11. 1 Kings
16. Nehemiah
19. Psalms

20.
17. Esther
20. Proverbs
22. Song of Solomon

21.
19. Psalms
21. Ecclesiastes
23. Isaiah

22.
17. Esther
21. Ecclesiastes
24. Jeremiah

23.
18. Job
22. Song of Solomon
25. Lamentations

24.
20. Proverbs
22. Song of Solomon
26. Ezekiel
29. Joel

25.
22. Song of Solomon
25. Lamentations
30. Amos

26.
23. Isaiah
26. Ezekiel
28. Hosea

27.
20. Proverbs
24. Jeremiah
27. Daniel
30. Amos

28.
22. Song of Solomon
25. Lamentations
29. Joel

29.
23. Isaiah
26. Ezekiel
27. Daniel
29. Joel

30.
20. Proverbs
24. Jeremiah
27. Daniel
30. Amos

31.
26. Ezekiel
29. Joel
32. Jonah
34. Nahum

32.
28. Hosea
31. Obadiah
33. Micah

33.
26. Ezekiel
31. Obadiah
34. Nahum

34.
27. Daniel
32. Jonah
35. Habakkuk

35.
32. Jonah
35. Habakkuk
37. Haggai

36.
33. Micah
36. Zephaniah
39. Malachi

37.
31. Obadiah
34. Nahum
37. Haggai
39. Malachi

38.
32. Jonah
35. Habakkuk
37. Haggai

39.
30. Amos
33. Micah
36. Zephaniah
38. Zechariah

40.
42. Luke

41.
40. Matthew
43. John

42.
41. Mark
44. Acts

43.
41. Mark
43. John
45. Romans
46. 1 Corinthians
47. 2 Corinthians
49. Ephesians

44.
44. Acts
47. 2 Corinthians
50. Philippians

45.
43. John
44. Acts
46. 1 Corinthians
48. Galatians

46.
45. Romans
48. Galatians
51. Colossians
53. 2 Thessalonians

47.
47. 2 Corinthians
49. Ephesians
51. Colossians
55. 2 Timothy

48.
50. Philippians
52. 1 Thessalonians

49.
49. Ephesians
51. Colossians
56. Titus
58. Hebrews

50.
50. Philippians
53. 2 Thessalonians
57. Philemon
59. James

51.
49. Ephesians
54. 1 Timothy
55. 2 Timothy
57. Philemon
59. James

52.
50. Philippians
51. Colossians
56. Titus
59. James

53.
53. 2 Thessalonians
57. Philemon
60. 1 Peter

54.
53. 2 Thessalonians
55. 2 Timothy
58. Hebrews

55.
59. James
62. 1 John

56.
55. 2 Timothy
56. Titus
60. 1 Peter
62. 1 John

57.
61. 2 Peter
64. 3 John

58.
58. Hebrews
60. 1 Peter
62. 1 John
64. 3 John

59.
59. James
65. Jude

60.
56. Titus
58. Hebrews
61. 2 Peter
64. 3 John
66. Revelation

5. The Ultimate Books of the Bible Test

1. Genesis
2. Leviticus
3. Deuteronomy
4. Ruth
5. 1 Samuel
6. 2 Kings
7. Ezra
8. Job
9. Ecclesiastes
10. Song of Solomon
11. Lamentations
12. Hosea
13. Amos
14. Obadiah
15. Micah
16. Habakkuk
17. Zechariah
18. Malachi
19. Matthew
20. Luke
21. Acts
22. 1 Corinthians
23. Ephesians
24. Colossians
25. 2 Thessalonians
26. 2 Timothy
27. James
28. 2 Peter
29. 3 John
30. Revelation

7. 200 Key Verses

1. believeth
2. Word
3. Father
4. nations
5. sinned
6. grace
7. beginning
8. power
9. All
10. Jesus
11. death
12. Repent
13. believe
14. good
15. Light
16. image
17. bodies
18. sinners
19. power
20. born
21. gospel
22. thief
23. Word
24. salvation
25. prayers
26. Spirit
27. Trust
28. evil
29. saved
30. world
31. troubled
32. baptized
33. evangelists
34. sin
35. rest
36. faith
37. created
38. gospel
39. cleanse
40. Pentecost
41. Christ
42. faith
43. approved
44. condemnation
45. saved
46. free
47. government
48. love
49. one
50. commandment
51. truth
52. Christ
53. sins
54. Father
55. darkness
56. spirit
57. Confess
58. virgin
59. believe
60. water
61. mind
62. sin
63. wrath
64. nothing
65. witnesses
66. made
67. rock
68. crucified
69. throne
70. fulfil
71. faith
72. righteousness

73. Spirit
74. truth
75. blood
76. salvation
77. truth
78. power
79. God
80. tables
81. baptized
82. righteous
83. woman
84. faith
85. Father
86. death
87. spirit
88. kind
89. joy
90. firstborn
91. mind
92. hope
93. praise
94. cloud
95. Samaria
96. humbly
97. Sanctify
98. Paul
99. house
100. resurrection
101. Abraham
102. tongues
103. branches
104. baptized

105. child
106. serpent
107. wisdom
108. prophets
109. truth's
110. eternal
111. water
112. disciples
113. instructed
114. voice
115. tasted
116. Father
117. hope
118. will
119. begotten
120. Abram
121. Spirit
122. vine
123. life
124. Let
125. light
126. chosen
127. sixth
128. judgment
129. Rabbi
130. light
131. Moses
132. deceived
133. life
134. Ask
135. Blessed
136. birth

137. excuse
138. Jesus
139. light
140. hope
141. forsake
142. spirit
143. gift
144. treasures
145. preach
146. one
147. promise
148. Jesus
149. sick
150. Son
151. principalities
152. pray
153. Repent
154. faith
155. LORD
156. saved
157. angel
158. fruitful
159. workmanship
160. sin
161. grace
162. salvation
163. death
164. brother
165. world
166. widows
167. overcome
168. graves

169. scriptures
170. women
171. worshippers
172. Judge
173. mediator
174. wilderness
175. God
176. prisoner
177. Spirit
178. submit
179. sea
180. coming
181. Father
182. disciples
183. lamp
184. man
185. fellowship
186. sins
187. wounded
188. redemption
189. church
190. flesh
191. love
192. Spirit
193. Moses
194. born
195. gate
196. deceiving
197. wife
198. sheep
199. created
200. Christ

9. The Ten Plagues Inflicted on Egypt

1.
1. Water turned into blood

2.
5. Death of livestock

3.
9. Darkness

4.
1. Water turned into blood
4. Flies
5. Death of livestock
8. Locusts
9. Darkness

5.
2. Frogs
3. Lice
6. Boils
7. Hailstorm

6.
2. Frogs
3. Lice
4. Flies
6. Boils
7. Hailstorm
9. Darkness

7.
1. Water turned into blood
2. Frogs
3. Lice
4. Flies
5. Death of livestock
6. Boils
7. Hailstorm
8. Locusts
9. Darkness
10. Death of all firstborn

10. Debt

1. Exodus 22:14
   And if a man <u>borrow</u> ought of his neighbour, and it be <u>hurt</u>, or <u>die</u>, the owner thereof being not with it, he shall surely make it <u>good</u>.
2. Deuteronomy 15:6
   For the LORD thy God blesseth thee, as he <u>promised</u> thee: and thou shalt lend unto many <u>nations</u>, but thou shalt not <u>borrow</u>; and thou shalt <u>reign</u> over many nations, but they shall not reign over thee.
3. Deuteronomy 28:12
   The LORD shall open unto thee his good <u>treasure</u>, the <u>heaven</u> to give the rain unto thy land in his <u>season</u>, and to bless all the work of thine <u>hand</u>: and thou shalt lend unto many <u>nations</u>, and thou shalt not borrow.
4. 2 Kings 4:7
   Then she came and told the man of <u>God</u>. And he said, Go, sell the <u>oil</u>, and pay thy <u>debt</u>, and live thou and thy <u>children</u> of the rest.
5. Psalm 37:21
   The wicked borroweth, and <u>payeth</u> not again: but the <u>righteous</u> sheweth <u>mercy</u>, and giveth.
6. Proverbs 22:7
   The <u>rich</u> ruleth over the <u>poor</u>, and the <u>borrower</u> is servant to the <u>lender</u>.
7. Proverbs 22:26–27
   Be not thou one of them that strike <u>hands</u>, or of them that are <u>sureties</u> for <u>debts</u>. If thou hast <u>nothing</u> to pay, why should he take away thy <u>bed</u> from under thee?
8. Ecclesiastes 5:5
   <u>Better</u> is it that thou shouldest not <u>vow</u>, than that thou shouldest vow and not <u>pay</u>.
9. Romans 13:8
   Owe no <u>man</u> any thing, but to love one <u>another</u>: for he that loveth another hath fulfilled the <u>law</u>.

11. Wealth

1. Exodus 23:12
   Six days thou shalt do thy work, and on the <u>seventh</u> day thou shalt rest: that thine <u>ox</u> and thine ass may rest, and the son of thy <u>handmaid</u>, and the <u>stranger</u>, may be <u>refreshed</u>.
2. Proverbs 12:11
   He that tilleth his <u>land</u> shall be satisfied with <u>bread</u>: but he that followeth <u>vain</u> persons is <u>void</u> of understanding.
3. Proverbs 13:11
   <u>Wealth</u> gotten by <u>vanity</u> shall be <u>diminished</u>: but he that gathereth by labour shall <u>increase</u>.
4. Proverbs 14:15
   The <u>simple</u> believeth every <u>word</u>: but the prudent <u>man</u> looketh <u>well</u> to his going.
5. Proverbs 19:2
   Also, that the soul be without <u>knowledge</u>, it is not <u>good</u>; and he that hasteth with his <u>feet</u> <u>sinneth</u>.
6. Proverbs 21:5
   The <u>thoughts</u> of the <u>diligent</u> <u>tend</u> only to plenteousness; but of <u>every</u> one that is <u>hasty</u> only to want.
7. Proverbs 23:4
   <u>Labour</u> not to be rich: cease from <u>thine</u> own <u>wisdom</u>.
8. Proverbs 28:19–20
   He that tilleth his land shall have plenty of <u>bread</u>: but he that followeth after <u>vain</u> persons shall have <u>poverty</u> enough. A faithful man shall abound with blessings: but he that maketh haste to be <u>rich</u> shall not be <u>innocent</u>.

12. Being Happy with What You Have

1. Psalm 23:1
   The LORD is my <u>shepherd</u>; I shall not <u>want</u>.
2. Ecclesiastes 5:10
   He that loveth <u>silver</u> shall not be satisfied with silver; nor he that loveth <u>abundance</u> with <u>increase</u>: this is also <u>vanity</u>.

3. Matthew 6:31–33
Therefore take no <u>thought</u>, saying, What shall we eat? or, What shall we <u>drink</u>? or, Wherewithal shall we be <u>clothed</u>? (For after all these things do the <u>Gentiles</u> seek:) for your heavenly Father knoweth that ye have need of all these things. But seek ye first the kingdom of God, and his <u>righteousness</u>; and all these things shall be added unto you.

4. Luke 3:14
And the <u>soldiers</u> likewise demanded of him, saying, And what shall we do? And he said unto them, Do <u>violence</u> to no man, neither accuse any <u>falsely</u>; and be content with your <u>wages</u>.

5. Philippians 4:11–13
Not that I speak in respect of want: for I have learned, in whatsoever <u>state</u> I am, therewith to be <u>content</u>. I know both how to be abased, and I know how to abound: every where and in all things I am <u>instructed</u> both to be full and to be <u>hungry</u>, both to abound and to suffer need. I can do all things through <u>Christ</u> which strengtheneth me.

6. 1 Thessalonians 4:11
And that ye study to be <u>quiet</u>, and to do your own <u>business</u>, and to work with your own <u>hands</u>, as we <u>commanded</u> you.

7. 1 Timothy 6:6
But <u>godliness</u> with <u>contentment</u> is great <u>gain</u>.

8. 1 Timothy 6:7–10
For we brought nothing into this world, and it is certain we can carry nothing out. And having food and <u>raiment</u> let us be therewith content. But they that will be rich fall into temptation and a snare, and into many <u>foolish</u> and hurtful <u>lusts</u>, which drown men in <u>destruction</u> and perdition. For the love of money is the root of all evil: which while some coveted after, they have erred from the <u>faith</u>, and pierced themselves through with many <u>sorrows</u>.

9. Hebrews 13:5
Let your <u>conversation</u> be without covetousness; and be content with such things as ye have: for he hath said, I will <u>never</u> leave thee, nor <u>forsake</u> thee.

10. James 4:1–3
From whence come <u>wars</u> and fightings among you? come they not hence, even of your lusts that <u>war</u> in your <u>members</u>? Ye lust, and have not: ye kill, and desire to have, and cannot obtain: ye fight and war, yet ye have not, because ye ask not. Ye <u>ask</u>, and receive not, because ye ask amiss, that ye may <u>consume</u> it upon your lusts.

13. Giving and Being Generous

1. Deuteronomy 15:10
Thou shalt surely give him, and thine <u>heart</u> shall not be grieved when thou givest unto him: because that for this thing the LORD thy God shall <u>bless</u> thee in all thy <u>works</u>, and in all that thou puttest thine <u>hand</u> unto.

2. Deuteronomy 16:17
Every <u>man</u> shall give as he is able, according to the <u>blessing</u> of the LORD thy <u>God</u> which he hath given <u>thee</u>.

3. 1 Chronicles 29:9
Then the <u>people</u> rejoiced, for that they offered willingly, because with perfect <u>heart</u> they offered willingly to the LORD: and <u>David</u> the <u>king</u> also rejoiced with great joy.

4. Proverbs 3:9–10
Honour the LORD with thy <u>substance</u>, and with the <u>firstfruits</u> of all thine increase: So shall thy <u>barns</u> be filled with plenty, and thy <u>presses</u> shall burst out with new <u>wine</u>.

5. Proverbs 3:27
Withhold not <u>good</u> from them to whom it is <u>due</u>, when it is in the <u>power</u> of thine <u>hand</u> to do it.

6. Proverbs 11:24–25
There is that <u>scattereth</u>, and yet <u>increaseth</u>; and there is that withholdeth more than is meet, but it tendeth to poverty. The liberal <u>soul</u> shall be made <u>fat</u>: and he that watereth shall be <u>watered</u> also himself.

7. Proverbs 21:26
He <u>coveteth</u> <u>greedily</u> all the <u>day</u> long: but the righteous giveth and <u>spareth</u> not.

8. Proverbs 22:9
He that hath a bountiful <u>eye</u> shall be <u>blessed</u>; for he giveth of his <u>bread</u> to the <u>poor</u>.

9. Proverbs 28:27
He that giveth unto the <u>poor</u> shall not <u>lack</u>:
but he that hideth his <u>eyes</u> shall have many
a <u>curse</u>.

10. Malachi 3:10
Bring ye all the tithes into the <u>storehouse</u>,
that there may be meat in mine house, and
prove me now herewith, saith the Lord of
hosts, if I will not open you the windows
of heaven, and pour you out a <u>blessing</u>,
that there shall not be <u>room</u> enough to
receive it.

11. Matthew 6:3–4
But when thou doest <u>alms</u>, let not thy left
<u>hand</u> know what thy right hand doeth:
That thine alms may be in <u>secret</u>: and thy
<u>Father</u> which seeth in secret himself shall
reward <u>thee</u> openly.

12. Mark 12:41–44
And Jesus sat over against the <u>treasury</u>,
and beheld how the people <u>cast</u> money
into the treasury: and many that were rich
cast in much. And there came a certain
poor widow, and she threw in two mites,
which make a farthing. And he called unto
him his disciples, and saith unto them,
Verily I say unto you, That this poor widow
hath cast more in, than all they which have
cast into the treasury: For all they did cast
in of their <u>abundance</u>; but she of her want
did cast in all that she had, even all her
<u>living</u>.

13. Luke 3:11
He <u>answereth</u> and saith unto them, He
that hath two <u>coats</u>, let him <u>impart</u> to him
that hath <u>none</u>; and he that hath <u>meat</u>, let
him do likewise.

14. Luke 6:30
Give to every <u>man</u> that asketh of <u>thee</u>;
and of him that taketh away thy <u>goods</u> ask
them not again.

15. Luke 6:38
Give, and it shall be given unto you; good
measure, pressed down, and <u>shaken</u> together, and <u>running</u> over, shall men give
into your <u>bosom</u>. For with the same measure that ye mete withal it shall be <u>mea-
sured</u> to you again.

16. Acts 20:35
I have shewed you all <u>things</u>, how that so
<u>labouring</u> ye ought to support the weak,
and to remember the words of the Lord
<u>Jesus</u>, how he said, It is more <u>blessed</u> to
give than to receive.

17. Romans 12:8
Or he that exhorteth, on <u>exhortation</u>: he
that giveth, let him do it with <u>simplicity</u>; he
that ruleth, with <u>diligence</u>; he that sheweth
mercy, with <u>cheerfulness</u>.

18. 2 Corinthians 9:6–8
But this I say, He which <u>soweth</u> sparingly
shall reap also sparingly; and he which
soweth bountifully shall reap also bountifully. Every man according as he purposeth
in his <u>heart</u>, so let him give; not <u>grudgingly</u>,
or of necessity: for God loveth a cheerful
giver. And God is able to make all grace
<u>abound</u> toward you; that ye, always having
all <u>sufficiency</u> in all things, may abound to
every good <u>work</u>.

19. 2 Corinthians 9:10
Now he that ministereth <u>seed</u> to the sower
both minister <u>bread</u> for your <u>food</u>, and
multiply your seed sown, and increase the
<u>fruits</u> of your righteousness.

20. Galatians 6:7
Be not deceived; <u>God</u> is not <u>mocked</u>: for
whatsoever a man <u>soweth</u>, that shall he
also <u>reap</u>.

21. Philippians 4:15–17
Now ye Philippians know also, that in the
beginning of the <u>gospel</u>, when I departed
from Macedonia, no <u>church</u> communicated with me as concerning giving and
receiving, but ye only. For even in Thessalonica ye sent once and again unto my
<u>necessity</u>. Not because I desire a gift: but
I desire <u>fruit</u> that may <u>abound</u> to your
<u>account</u>.

22. James 2:15–16
If a brother or <u>sister</u> be naked, and destitute of daily <u>food</u>, And one of you say
unto them, Depart in peace, be ye warmed
and <u>filled</u>; notwithstanding ye give them
not those things which are needful to the
<u>body</u>; what doth it <u>profit</u>?

14. Receiving

1. Ecclesiastes 5:19
Every man also to whom <u>God</u> hath given riches and wealth, and hath given him power to eat thereof, and to take his <u>portion</u>, and to rejoice in his <u>labour</u>; this is the <u>gift</u> of God.

2. John 3:27
<u>John</u> answered and said, A <u>man</u> can receive <u>nothing</u>, except it be given him from <u>heaven</u>.

3. Acts 20:35
I have shewed you all things, how that so <u>labouring</u> ye ought to support the <u>weak</u>, and to remember the <u>words</u> of the Lord Jesus, how he said, It is more <u>blessed</u> to give than to receive.

4. 1 Corinthians 9:10–11
Or saith he it altogether for our sakes? For our sakes, no doubt, this is <u>written</u>: that he that <u>ploweth</u> should plow in hope; and that he that <u>thresheth</u> in hope should be partaker of his hope. If we have sown unto you spiritual <u>things</u>, is it a great thing if we shall reap your <u>carnal</u> things?

5. 1 Timothy 5:18
For the <u>scripture</u> saith, thou shalt not <u>muzzle</u> the <u>ox</u> that treadeth out the corn. And, The <u>labourer</u> is worthy of his <u>reward</u>.

15. Running a Business

1. Leviticus 19:13
<u>Thou</u> shalt not defraud thy <u>neighbour</u>, neither rob him: the <u>wages</u> of him that is hired shall not abide with <u>thee</u> all night until the <u>morning</u>.

2. Deuteronomy 25:13–15
Thou shalt not have in thy <u>bag</u> divers weights, a <u>great</u> and a small. Thou shalt not have in thine house divers measures, a great and a small. But thou shalt have a <u>perfect</u> and just <u>weight</u>, a perfect and just <u>measure</u> shalt thou have: that thy days may be lengthened in the land which the Lord thy <u>God</u> giveth thee.

3. Job 31:13–14
If I did despise the cause of my <u>manservant</u> or of my maidservant, when they contended with me; What then shall I do when God <u>riseth</u> up? and when he <u>visiteth</u>, what shall I answer him?

4. Psalm 112:5
A good man sheweth <u>favour</u>, and <u>lendeth</u>: he will guide his <u>affairs</u> with <u>discretion</u>.

5. Proverbs 10:4
He becometh <u>poor</u> that <u>dealeth</u> with a slack <u>hand</u>: but the hand of the <u>diligent</u> maketh rich.

6. Proverbs 11:1
A false <u>balance</u> is <u>abomination</u> to the Lord: but a just weight is his <u>delight</u>.

7. Proverbs 13:4
The <u>soul</u> of the <u>sluggard</u> desireth, and hath <u>nothing</u>: but the soul of the diligent shall be made <u>fat</u>.

8. Proverbs 13:11
<u>Wealth</u> gotten by <u>vanity</u> shall be diminished: but he that gathereth by <u>labour</u> shall <u>increase</u>.

9. Proverbs 16:8
<u>Better</u> is a little with <u>righteousness</u> than great <u>revenues</u> without <u>right</u>.

10. Proverbs 22:16
He that <u>oppresseth</u> the <u>poor</u> to increase his <u>riches</u>, and he that giveth to the <u>rich</u>, shall surely come to want.

11. Jeremiah 22:13
Woe unto him that <u>buildeth</u> his house by unrighteousness, and his chambers by wrong; that useth his neighbour's <u>service</u> without <u>wages</u>, and giveth him not for his <u>work</u>.

12. Malachi 3:5
And I will come near to you to judgment; and I will be a swift witness against the sorcerers, and against the <u>adulterers</u>, and against false <u>swearers</u>, and against those that oppress the <u>hireling</u> in his wages, the widow, and the fatherless, and that turn aside the stranger from his right, and <u>fear</u> not me, saith the Lord of <u>hosts</u>.

13. Luke 16:10
    He that is faithful in that which is <u>least</u> is <u>faithful</u> also in much: and he that is <u>unjust</u> in the least is unjust also in <u>much</u>.

14. Ephesians 6:9
    And, ye masters, do the same <u>things</u> unto them, forbearing threatening: knowing that your <u>Master</u> also is in <u>heaven</u>; neither is there respect of <u>persons</u> with him.

15. Colossians 4:1
    <u>Masters</u>, give unto your <u>servants</u> that which is just and equal; knowing that ye also have a <u>Master</u> in <u>heaven</u>.

16. James 5:4
    Behold, the hire of the <u>labourers</u> who have reaped down your <u>fields</u>, which is of you kept back by <u>fraud</u>, crieth: and the <u>cries</u> of them which have reaped are entered into the ears of the <u>Lord</u> of sabaoth.

16. God's Provisions

1. 1 Kings 17:13–16
   And Elijah said unto her, Fear not; go and do as thou hast said: but make me thereof a little cake first, and bring it unto me, and after make for thee and for thy <u>son</u>. For thus saith the LORD God of <u>Israel</u>, The barrel of meal shall not waste, neither shall the cruse of oil fail, until the day that the LORD sendeth rain upon the earth. And she went and did according to the saying of <u>Elijah</u>: and she, and he, and her <u>house</u>, did eat many days. And the barrel of <u>meal</u> wasted not, neither did the cruse of oil fail, according to the word of the LORD, which he spake by Elijah.

2. Nehemiah 6:9
   For they all made us <u>afraid</u>, saying, Their <u>hands</u> shall be <u>weakened</u> from the work, that it be not done. Now <u>therefore</u>, O God, strengthen my hands.

3. Psalm 37:25
   I have been <u>young</u>, and now am <u>old</u>; yet have I not seen the righteous forsaken, nor his <u>seed</u> begging <u>bread</u>.

4. Matthew 6:31–32
   Therefore take no thought, saying, What shall we eat? or, What shall we drink? or, Wherewithal shall we be <u>clothed</u>? (For after all these things do the <u>Gentiles</u> seek:) for your heavenly <u>Father</u> knoweth that ye have need of all these <u>things</u>.

5. Matthew 7:11
   If ye then, being <u>evil</u>, know how to give good gifts unto your <u>children</u>, how much more shall your <u>Father</u> which is in <u>heaven</u> give good things to them that ask him?

6. Luke 12:7
   But even the very <u>hairs</u> of your <u>head</u> are all <u>numbered</u>. Fear not therefore: ye are of more <u>value</u> than many <u>sparrows</u>.

7. John 21:6
   And he said unto them, <u>cast</u> the <u>net</u> on the <u>right</u> side of the <u>ship</u>, and ye shall find. They cast therefore, and now they were not able to draw it for the multitude of <u>fishes</u>.

8. 2 Corinthians 9:8
   And God is able to make all <u>grace</u> abound toward you; that ye, always having <u>all</u> <u>sufficiency</u> in all things, may <u>abound</u> to every good <u>work</u>.

9. Philippians 4:19
   But my <u>God</u> shall supply all your need according to his <u>riches</u> in <u>glory</u> by Christ <u>Jesus</u>.

17. Lending

1. Exodus 22:25
   If thou lend <u>money</u> to any of my <u>people</u> that is poor by thee, <u>thou</u> shalt not be to him as an usurer, neither shalt thou lay upon him <u>usury</u>.

2. Leviticus 25:35–37
   And if thy brother be <u>waxen</u> poor, and fallen in <u>decay</u> with thee; then thou shalt relieve him: yea, though he be a stranger, or a <u>sojourner</u>; that he may live with thee. Take thou no usury of him, or increase: but fear thy God; that thy <u>brother</u> may live with thee. Thou shalt not give him thy <u>money</u> upon usury, nor lend him thy <u>victuals</u> for increase.

3. Deuteronomy 15:8
   But thou shalt open thine <u>hand</u> wide unto him, and shalt surely lend him <u>sufficient</u> for his <u>need</u>, in that which he <u>wanteth</u>.

4. Deuteronomy 23:19–20
Thou shalt not <u>lend</u> upon usury to thy
<u>brother</u>; usury of money, usury of victuals,
usury of any thing that is lent upon usury:
Unto a <u>stranger</u> thou mayest lend upon
usury; but unto thy brother thou shalt not
lend upon usury: that the LORD thy <u>God</u>
may <u>bless</u> thee in all that thou settest thine
<u>hand</u> to in the land whither thou goest to
possess it.

5. Deuteronomy 24:10
When thou dost <u>lend</u> thy <u>brother</u> any
thing, thou shalt not go into his <u>house</u> to
fetch his <u>pledge</u>.

6. Psalm 15:5
He that putteth not out his <u>money</u> to
<u>usury</u>, nor taketh reward against the <u>in-
nocent</u>. He that doeth these <u>things</u> shall
never be <u>moved</u>.

7. Psalm 37:26
<u>He</u> is ever <u>merciful</u>, and lendeth; and his
<u>seed</u> is <u>blessed</u>.

8. Psalm 112:5
A good <u>man</u> <u>sheweth</u> favour, and <u>lendeth</u>:
he will guide his affairs with <u>discretion</u>.

9. Proverbs 3:27–28
Withhold not good from them to whom
it is due, when it is in the <u>power</u> of thine
<u>hand</u> to do it. Say not unto thy <u>neighbour</u>,
Go, and come again, and to morrow I will
give; when thou hast it by <u>thee</u>.

10. Proverbs 28:8
He that by <u>usury</u> and unjust gain <u>increas-
eth</u> his <u>substance</u>, he shall gather it for him
that will pity the <u>poor</u>.

11. Matthew 5:42
Give to him that <u>asketh</u> <u>thee</u>, and from
him that would <u>borrow</u> of thee turn not
<u>thou</u> away.

12. Luke 6:35
But love ye your <u>enemies</u>, and do good,
and lend, hoping for <u>nothing</u> again; and
your reward shall be <u>great</u>, and ye shall be
the <u>children</u> of the <u>Highest</u>: for he is kind
unto the unthankful and to the <u>evil</u>.

18. Being Truly Prosperous

1. Genesis 26:12
Then Isaac sowed in that <u>land</u>, and received in the same <u>year</u> an <u>hundredfold</u>:
and the LORD <u>blessed</u> him.

2. Genesis 39:3
And his <u>master</u> saw that the LORD was with
him, and that the <u>LORD</u> made all that he
did to <u>prosper</u> in his <u>hand</u>.

3. Deuteronomy 8:18
But thou shalt <u>remember</u> the LORD thy
God: for it is he that giveth thee <u>power</u> to
get <u>wealth</u>, that he may establish his <u>cov-
enant</u> which he sware unto thy <u>fathers</u>, as
it is this day.

4. Deuteronomy 15:10
<u>Thou</u> shalt surely give him, and thine heart
shall not be <u>grieved</u> when thou givest unto
him: because that for this thing the LORD
thy God shall <u>bless</u> thee in all thy <u>works</u>,
and in all that thou puttest thine <u>hand</u>
unto.

5. Deuteronomy 24:19
When thou cuttest down thine <u>harvest</u>
in thy field, and hast forgot a <u>sheaf</u> in the
field, thou shalt not go again to <u>fetch</u> it:
it shall be for the stranger, for the fatherless, and for the widow: that the <u>LORD</u> thy

God may bless thee in all the <u>work</u> of thine
hands.

6. Deuteronomy 30:8–10
And thou shalt return and obey the voice
of the LORD, and do all his commandments
which I command thee this day. And the
LORD thy God will make thee plenteous in
every <u>work</u> of thine hand, in the fruit of
thy body, and in the fruit of thy <u>cattle</u>, and
in the fruit of thy land, for good: for the
LORD will again rejoice over thee for good,
as he rejoiced over thy <u>fathers</u>: If thou
shalt hearken unto the <u>voice</u> of the LORD
thy God, to keep his <u>commandments</u> and
his statutes which are written in this book
of the law, and if thou turn unto the LORD
thy God with all thine heart, and with all
thy <u>soul</u>.

7. Joshua 1:8
This book of the law shall not depart out
of thy <u>mouth</u>; but thou shalt meditate
therein day and <u>night</u>, that thou mayest
observe to do according to all that is <u>writ-
ten</u> therein: for then thou shalt make thy
way prosperous, and then thou shalt have
good <u>success</u>.

8. 1 Chronicles 22:12
Only the LORD give thee wisdom and understanding, and give thee <u>charge</u> concerning Israel, that thou mayest keep the <u>law</u> of the LORD thy <u>God</u>.

9. 2 Chronicles 31:20
And thus did <u>Hezekiah</u> throughout all <u>Judah</u>, and wrought that which was good and right and truth before the LORD his <u>God</u>.

10. Psalm 1:1–3
Blessed is the man that walketh not in the counsel of the <u>ungodly</u>, nor standeth in the way of sinners, nor sitteth in the seat of the <u>scornful</u>. But his delight is in the law of the LORD; and in his law doth he meditate day and night. And he shall be like a <u>tree</u> planted by the rivers of <u>water</u>, that bringeth forth his fruit in his season; his leaf also shall not wither; and whatsoever he doeth shall <u>prosper</u>.

11. Psalm 35:27
Let them shout for joy, and be glad, that favour my <u>righteous</u> cause: yea, let them say continually, Let the LORD be <u>magnified</u>, which hath pleasure in the <u>prosperity</u> of his <u>servant</u>.

12. Jeremiah 17:8
For he shall be as a <u>tree</u> planted by the <u>waters</u>, and that spreadeth out her roots by the <u>river</u>, and shall not see when heat cometh, but her leaf shall be <u>green</u>; and shall not be careful in the year of <u>drought</u>, neither shall cease from yielding fruit.

13. Malachi 3:10
Bring ye all the <u>tithes</u> into the storehouse, that there may be meat in mine <u>house</u>, and prove me now herewith, saith the LORD of <u>hosts</u>, if I will not open you the windows of <u>heaven</u>, and pour you out a <u>blessing</u>, that there shall not be room enough to receive it.

14. 3 John 1:2
<u>Beloved</u>, I wish above all things that thou mayest <u>prosper</u> and be in <u>health</u>, even as thy <u>soul</u> prospereth.

19. Being a Good Steward over One's Money

1. Genesis 2:15
And the LORD God <u>took</u> the <u>man</u>, and put him into the <u>garden</u> of <u>Eden</u> to dress it and to <u>keep</u> it.

2. Deuteronomy 10:14
<u>Behold</u>, the <u>heaven</u> and the heaven of <u>heavens</u> is the LORD's thy God, the <u>earth</u> also, with all that therein is.

3. Luke 12:42–44
And the Lord said, Who then is that faithful and wise <u>steward</u>, whom his lord shall make <u>ruler</u> over his <u>household</u>, to give them their portion of <u>meat</u> in due season? Blessed is that <u>servant</u>, whom his lord when he cometh shall find so doing. Of a truth I say unto you, that he will make him ruler over all that he hath.

4. Luke 12:47–48
And that <u>servant</u>, which knew his lord's will, and prepared not himself, neither did according to his will, shall be beaten with many stripes. But he that knew not, and did commit things worthy of <u>stripes</u>, shall be <u>beaten</u> with few stripes. For unto <u>whomsoever</u> much is given, of him shall be much required: and to whom men have <u>committed</u> much, of him they will ask the more.

5. Luke 16:9–11
And I say unto you, Make to yourselves <u>friends</u> of the mammon of unrighteousness; that, when ye fail, they may receive you into everlasting habitations. He that is faithful in that which is least is <u>faithful</u> also in much: and he that is <u>unjust</u> in the least is unjust also in much. If therefore ye have not been faithful in the unrighteous <u>mammon</u>, who will commit to your trust the true <u>riches</u>?

6. Romans 14:8
For whether we live, we live unto the Lord; and whether we <u>die</u>, we die unto the <u>Lord</u>: whether we <u>live</u> therefore, or die, we are the <u>Lord's</u>.

20. Saving

1. Proverbs 21:5
   The <u>thoughts</u> of the diligent <u>tend</u> only to plenteousness; but of every one that is <u>hasty</u> only to <u>want</u>.
2. Proverbs 21:20
   There is <u>treasure</u> to be desired and <u>oil</u> in the dwelling of the <u>wise</u>; but a foolish man <u>spendeth</u> it up.
3. Proverbs 27:12
   A <u>prudent</u> man foreseeth the <u>evil</u>, and hideth himself; but the <u>simple</u> pass on, and are <u>punished</u>.
4. Proverbs 30:25
   The ants are a <u>people</u> not strong, yet they prepare their meat in the <u>summer</u>.
5. 1 Corinthians 16:2
   Upon the first <u>day</u> of the <u>week</u> let every one of you lay by him in store, as <u>God</u> hath prospered him, that there be no <u>gatherings</u> when I come.

21. Tithing

1. Genesis 14:20
   And blessed be the most high <u>God</u>, which hath delivered <u>thine</u> enemies into thy <u>hand</u>. And he gave him <u>tithes</u> of all.
2. Genesis 28:20–22
   And <u>Jacob</u> vowed a vow, saying, If God will be with me, and will keep me in this way that I go, and will give me <u>bread</u> to eat, and raiment to put on, So that I come again to my father's <u>house</u> in peace; then shall the LORD be my God: And this stone, which I have set for a <u>pillar</u>, shall be God's house: and of all that thou shalt give me I will surely give the <u>tenth</u> unto thee.
3. Exodus 23:19
   The first of the <u>firstfruits</u> of thy <u>land</u> thou shalt bring into the <u>house</u> of the LORD thy God. Thou shalt not seethe a <u>kid</u> in his mother's <u>milk</u>.
4. Leviticus 27:30
   And all the <u>tithe</u> of the <u>land</u>, whether of the <u>seed</u> of the land, or of the fruit of the tree, is the LORD's: it is holy unto the LORD.
5. Numbers 18:26
   Thus speak unto the <u>Levites</u>, and say unto them, When ye take of the children of <u>Israel</u> the tithes which I have given you from them for your <u>inheritance</u>, then ye shall offer up an heave offering of it for the LORD, even a tenth part of the <u>tithe</u>.
6. Deuteronomy 14:22-23
   Thou shalt truly <u>tithe</u> all the increase of thy seed, that the field bringeth forth <u>year</u> by year. And thou shalt eat before the LORD thy God, in the place which he shall choose to place his <u>name</u> there, the tithe of thy <u>corn</u>, of thy wine, and of thine oil, and the <u>firstlings</u> of thy herds and of thy <u>flocks</u>; that thou mayest learn to fear the LORD thy God always.
7. Deuteronomy 14:28
   At the end of <u>three</u> <u>years</u> thou shalt bring forth all the tithe of thine <u>increase</u> the same <u>year</u>, and shalt lay it up within thy <u>gates</u>.
8. Deuteronomy 26:12
   When thou hast made an end of <u>tithing</u> all the tithes of thine increase the third year, which is the year of tithing, and hast given it unto the <u>Levite</u>, the <u>stranger</u>, the <u>fatherless</u>, and the <u>widow</u>, that they may eat within thy gates, and be filled.
9. 2 Chronicles 31:5
   And as soon as the <u>commandment</u> came abroad, the children of <u>Israel</u> brought in abundance the firstfruits of corn, <u>wine</u>, and oil, and honey, and of all the increase of the field; and the <u>tithe</u> of all things brought they in <u>abundantly</u>.
10. Nehemiah 10:38
    And the priest the son of <u>Aaron</u> shall be with the <u>Levites</u>, when the Levites take <u>tithes</u>: and the Levites shall bring up the tithe of the tithes unto the <u>house</u> of our God, to the chambers, into the <u>treasure</u> house.
11. Proverbs 3:9–10
    Honour the LORD with thy substance, and with the firstfruits of all thine increase: So shall thy <u>barns</u> be filled with <u>plenty</u>, and thy presses shall burst out with new <u>wine</u>.

12. Ezekiel 44:30
And the first of all the <u>firstfruits</u> of all
things, and every oblation of all, of every
sort of your oblations, shall be the priest's:
ye shall also give unto the <u>priest</u> the first of
your <u>dough</u>, that he may cause the <u>bless-
ing</u> to rest in thine house.

13. Amos 4:4
Come to <u>Bethel</u>, and transgress; at Gilgal
multiply <u>transgression</u>; and bring your <u>sac-
rifices</u> every morning, and your <u>tithes</u> after
three years.

14. Malachi 3:8
Will a man <u>rob</u> God? Yet ye have <u>robbed</u>
me. But ye say, Wherein have we robbed
<u>thee</u>? In <u>tithes</u> and <u>offerings</u>.

15. Matthew 23:23
Woe unto you, scribes and <u>Pharisees</u>,
hypocrites! for ye pay tithe of mint and
anise and <u>cummin</u>, and have omitted the
<u>weightier</u> matters of the law, <u>judgment</u>,
mercy, and faith: these ought ye to have
done, and not to leave the other <u>undone</u>.

16. 1 Corinthians 16:1–2
Now concerning the collection for
the <u>saints</u>, as I have given order to the
<u>churches</u> of <u>Galatia</u>, even so do ye. Upon
the first day of the <u>week</u> let every one of
you lay by him in store, as <u>God</u> hath prospered him, that there be no gatherings
when I come.

17. Hebrews 7:4
Now consider how great this <u>man</u> was,
unto whom even the <u>patriarch</u> <u>Abraham</u>
gave the tenth of the <u>spoils</u>.

22. All about Food

1. C (Matthew 3:4)
2. D (Genesis 25:34)
3. B (Genesis 40)
4. C (Genesis 27)
5. B (Ezekiel 3:3)
6. A (Judges 6:19)
7. B (Exodus 3:17)
8. D (Luke 15:22–24)
9. C (Numbers 11:4–5)
10. D (Judges 14:8–10)
11. B (2 Kings 4:38–41)
12. B (Exodus 16:31)

23. From Sweet to Bitter

1. D (Revelation 10:8–10)
2. C (Judges 14:12–14)
3. A (Proverbs 20:16–18)
4. C (Jeremiah 31:28–30)
5. C (Exodus 12:8)
6. D (Proverbs 9:17)
7. A (Exodus 15:23–25)
8. D (Mark 16:18)
9. D (Exodus 32:20)
10. C (Proverbs 27:7)

24. Kiddie Land

1. A (Genesis 4:1)
2. C (Genesis 9:22–24)
3. B (1 Samuel 16:6–13)
4. B (Genesis 48:13–14)
5. D (1 Kings 16:28–30)
6. B (Genesis 35:16–19)
7. B (Judges 8:30)
8. A (2 Chronicles 11:21)
9. B (1 Corinthians 14:20)
10. C (2 Samuel 17:14–17; 18:33)

26. That Makes Scents

1. B (Matthew 2:11)
2. D (Esther 2:12–14)
3. C (John 12:3)
4. A (Luke 7:36)
5. C (Song of Solomon 4:13–15)
6. B (Proverbs 7:17)
7. A (Song of Solomon 3:6–7)
8. B (Daniel 10:2–3)
9. B (Proverbs 27:9)
10. D (Jeremiah 4:30; Eze-kiel 23:40)

27. Wedding Bells

1. B (Genesis 4:19)
2. D (Genesis 29:1–35)
3. B (1 Samuel 1:1–2)
4. B (1 Samuel 14:50)
5. B (Ruth 4:8–10)
6. D (Genesis 38:1–30)
7. A (2 Chronicles 13:21)
8. A (Judges 14:20)

28. Farming

1. D (Genesis 2:8)
2. B (Job 1:1–22)
3. D (Ecclesiastes 2:4–5)
4. A (Judges 6:11)
5. D (Genesis 9:20)
6. C (Ruth 1:22–2:3; 4:13–17)
7. B (Genesis 26:12)
8. A (2 Chronicles 26:9–10)
9. B (1 Kings 21:1–4)
10. C (2 Samuel 9:1–13)

29. Rulers

1. C (1 Kings 3:16–28)
2. B (1 Kings 2:11)
3. D (Matthew 2:16–18)
4. C (Daniel 6:1–16)
5. A (1 Kings 15:23)
6. B (1 Samuel 16:11–13)
7. C (Genesis 41:1–40)
8. B (1 Kings 3:1)
9. C (Joshua 12:7–24)
10. A (Numbers 22:2–7)
11. C (Judges 9:1–6)
12. B (1 Samuel 15:1–35)
13. A (1 Samuel 21:10)

30. The Apostles

1. C (Matthew 10:2)
2. B (Matthew 17:1–3)
3. C (Acts 9:32–34)
4. A (John 12:20–22)

31. In the Military

1. C (Acts 12:5–8)
2. D (2 Kings 5:1)
3. B (Luke 7:1–5)
4. B (Acts 27:1–3)
5. C (Joshua 14:6–13)
6. C (2 Samuel 11:3, 14–15)
7. B (2 Samuel 15:14–22)
8. C (1 Kings 16:8–10)
9. B (2 Samuel 17:25)

32. Women and Rulers

1. C (2 Samuel 11:27; 12:24)
2. B (2 Samuel 21:11)
3. C (Matthew 14:3–8)
4. B (1 Kings 16:31)
5. C (1 Kings 10:1–2)
6. C (Esther 1:11–12; 2:17)
7. B (1 Samuel 25:39–42)
8. A (2 Chronicles 15:16)
9. B (Acts 8:27)
10. D (2 Chronicles 22:10)

33. Hair Apparent

1. C (Judges 16:17–19)
2. B (Acts 21:23–26)
3. B (Daniel 4:33)
4. C (Genesis 25:24–26)
5. C (2 Kings 1:8)
6. D (Job 1:20)
7. C (Leviticus 19:27)
8. C (2 Kings 2:22–23)
9. C (Leviticus 14:7–9)
10. C (Ezekiel 44:15–20)
11. C (Ezekiel 1:1–3; 5:1–4)

34. Anointment

1. D (Acts 10:38)
2. C (Exodus 40:1–9)
3. B (Genesis 28:18)
4. D (2 Corinthians 1:22)
5. C (Leviticus 8:23–24)
6. D (1 Samuel 9:15–16; 10:1)
7. C (James 5:14)
8. B (Isaiah 45:1)
9. B (1 Kings 1:39)

35. The Swift

1. C (1 Samuel 17:48–49)
2. C (Luke 19:2–4)
3. A (Genesis 33:4)
4. C (1 Kings 18:44–46)
5. B (Genesis 17:1; 18:1–3)
6. C (Genesis 24:27–29)
7. A (2 Samuel 18:21)
8. A (1 Kings 1:5)
9. D (2 Kings 4:8–37)

36. Special Women

1. A (Judges 4:3–5)
2. A (Luke 1:34–36, 57–60)
3. B (Exodus 15:20)
4. C (Esther 1–10)
5. D (1 Kings 16:31–34)
6. C (1 Samuel 25:1–42)
7. D (Joshua 6:25)
8. D (2 Samuel 3:2–5)
9. A (2 Samuel 21:8–10)
10. C (2 Kings 22:14–20)

37. Fly High

1. B (James 3:7–8)
2. C (Matthew 3:16)
3. D (Genesis 7:2–3)
4. A (Revelation 1:1–2; 12:14)
5. B (Exodus 16:13)
6. C (Mark 4:1–4)

38. What's That I Hear?

1. A (Acts 2:1–14)
2. A (Revelation 1:1–2; 18:1–3)
3. B (Matthew 3:16–17)
4. C (Revelation 1:1–2; 6:10)
5. C (1 Kings 19:1–21)
6. D (1 Samuel 3:2–4)
7. C (Psalm 29:5)
8. D (2 Kings 19:14–22)
9. C (1 Samuel 28:7–12)

40. The Story of Joseph

1. B (Genesis 42:3)
2. B (Genesis 42:4)
3. A (Genesis 42:17)
4. D (Genesis 42:18–24)
5. A (Genesis 42:25)
6. B (Genesis 44:2)
7. C (Genesis 44:17)
8. B (Genesis 47:1–6)
9. B (Genesis 45:18)
10. C (Genesis 50:26)
11. D (Genesis 41:51)
12. C (Genesis 45:22)

41. Have a Laugh

1. B (Matthew 9:23–24)
2. C (Genesis 17:17)
3. A (2 Samuel 6:12–14)
4. D (Genesis 18:12)
5. A (Exodus 32:4, 19)
6. D (Genesis 21:6)
7. C (Luke 6:21)
8. D (Judges 11:34)
9. C (1 Samuel 30:16–19)
10. A (Nehemiah 2:19)

42. Priests

1. C (Deuteronomy 17:12)
2. B (Exodus 28:15–21)
3. B (Hebrews 7:1–3)
4. B (Hebrews 7:1–3)
5. A (1 Samuel 1:12–14)
6. D (2 Kings 23:1–30)
7. C (1 Samuel 2:12–17, 34)
8. B (Exodus 18:13–27)

43. Lions' Den

1. C (Revelation 1:1–2; 4:6–7)
2. D (Daniel 7:2–4)
3. C (1 Samuel 17:34–35)
4. A (1 Peter 5:8)
5. B (Judges 14:5–6)
6. B (2 Samuel 1:23)
7. C (Ezekiel 1:1–10)
8. D (2 Samuel 23:20)

45. Scriptures on Assurance

1. Genesis 1:1
In the <u>beginning</u> God created the <u>heaven</u> and the <u>earth</u>.
2. Psalm 37:4
Delight <u>thyself</u> also in the LORD: and he shall give thee the <u>desires</u> of thine <u>heart</u>.
3. Isaiah 9:6
For unto us a <u>child</u> is born, unto us a son is given: and the <u>government</u> shall be upon his shoulder: and his name shall be called <u>Wonderful</u>, Counsellor, The mighty God, The everlasting Father, The Prince of Peace.
4. Isaiah 40:28
Hast thou not <u>known</u>? hast thou not heard, that the <u>everlasting</u> God, the LORD, the Creator of the ends of the earth, fainteth not, neither is <u>weary</u>? there is no searching of his understanding.
5. Jeremiah 29:11
For I know the <u>thoughts</u> that I think toward you, saith the LORD, thoughts of peace, and not of <u>evil</u>, to give you an expected end.
6. John 3:16
For God so <u>loved</u> the <u>world</u>, that he gave his only begotten <u>Son</u>, that whosoever believeth in him should not perish, but have everlasting <u>life</u>.
7. John 15:7
If ye <u>abide</u> in me, and my words abide in you, ye shall ask what ye <u>will</u>, and it shall be done unto <u>you</u>.
8. Romans 4:21
And being <u>fully</u> persuaded that, what he had <u>promised</u>, he was able also to <u>perform</u>.

9. Romans 8:1
There is therefore now no <u>condemnation</u> to them which are in Christ <u>Jesus</u>, who walk not after the flesh, but after the <u>Spirit</u>.
10. Romans 8:28
And we know that all things <u>work</u> together for <u>good</u> to them that <u>love</u> God, to them who are the called according to his <u>purpose</u>.
11. 2 Corinthians 1:20
For all the <u>promises</u> of God in him are yea, and in him <u>Amen</u>, unto the <u>glory</u> of God by us.
12. Ephesians 2:10
For we are his workmanship, created in Christ Jesus unto good <u>works</u>, which God hath before <u>ordained</u> that we should walk in them.
13. Philippians 4:6–7
Be careful for <u>nothing</u>; but in every thing by <u>prayer</u> and supplication with <u>thanksgiving</u> let your requests be made known unto God. And the peace of God, which passeth all understanding, shall keep your hearts and <u>minds</u> through Christ Jesus.
14. Philippians 4:19
But my God shall <u>supply</u> all your need according to his <u>riches</u> in <u>glory</u> by Christ Jesus.
15. 2 Peter 1:4
Whereby are given unto us exceeding <u>great</u> and precious <u>promises</u>: that by these ye might be partakers of the divine <u>nature</u>, having escaped the corruption that is in the world through lust.

46. Scriptures on Salvation

1. John 14:6
Jesus saith unto him, I am the <u>way</u>, the truth, and the <u>life</u>: no man cometh unto the <u>Father</u>, but by me.
2. Romans 3:23
For all have <u>sinned</u>, and come short of the <u>glory</u> of God.
3. Romans 6:23
For the wages of <u>sin</u> is <u>death</u>; but the gift of God is eternal <u>life</u> through Jesus Christ our Lord.

4. 2 Corinthians 5:17
Therefore if any man be in <u>Christ</u>, he is a new <u>creature</u>: old things are passed away; behold, all things are become <u>new</u>.
5. Ephesians 2:8–9
For by <u>grace</u> are ye saved through <u>faith</u>; and that not of yourselves: it is the gift of God: Not of works, lest any man should <u>boast</u>.
6. Revelation 3:20
Behold, I stand at the <u>door</u>, and <u>knock</u>: if any man hear my <u>voice</u>, and open the door, I will come in to him, and will sup with him, and he with me.

47. Scriptures on Security

1. Psalm 27:1
   The Lord is my light and my salvation; whom shall I fear? the Lord is the strength of my life; of whom shall I be afraid?

2. Psalm 37:4
   Delight thyself also in the Lord: and he shall give thee the desires of thine heart.

3. Proverbs 3:5–6
   Trust in the Lord with all thine heart; and lean not unto thine own understanding. In all thy ways acknowledge him, and he shall direct thy paths.

4. Isaiah 40:31
   But they that wait upon the Lord shall renew their strength; they shall mount up with wings as eagles; they shall run, and not be weary; and they shall walk, and not faint.

5. Jeremiah 29:11
   For I know the thoughts that I think toward you, saith the Lord, thoughts of peace, and not of evil, to give you an expected end.

6. Lamentations 3:22–23
   It is of the Lord's mercies that we are not consumed, because his compassions fail not. They are new every morning: great is thy faithfulness.

7. Matthew 11:28–30
   Come unto me, all ye that labour and are heavy laden, and I will give you rest. Take my yoke upon you, and learn of me; for I am meek and lowly in heart: and ye shall find rest unto your souls. For my yoke is easy, and my burden is light.

8. Luke 16:13
   No servant can serve two masters: for either he will hate the one, and love the other; or else he will hold to the one, and despise the other. Ye cannot serve God and mammon.

9. Acts 1:8
   But ye shall receive power, after that the Holy Ghost is come upon you: and ye shall be witnesses unto me both in Jerusalem, and in all Judaea, and in Samaria, and unto the uttermost part of the earth.

10. Romans 8:28
    And we know that all things work together for good to them that love God, to them who are the called according to his purpose.

11. Romans 8:38–39
    For I am persuaded, that neither death, nor life, nor angels, nor principalities, nor powers, nor things present, nor things to come, Nor height, nor depth, nor any other creature, shall be able to separate us from the love of God, which is in Christ Jesus our Lord.

12. Romans 12:1
    I beseech you therefore, brethren, by the mercies of God, that ye present your bodies a living sacrifice, holy, acceptable unto God, which is your reasonable service.

13. 1 Corinthians 15:58
    Therefore, my beloved brethren, be ye stedfast, unmoveable, always abounding in the work of the Lord, forasmuch as ye know that your labour is not in vain in the Lord.

14. 2 Corinthians 4:18
    While we look not at the things which are seen, but at the things which are not seen: for the things which are seen are temporal; but the things which are not seen are eternal.

15. 2 Corinthians 12:9
    And he said unto me, My grace is sufficient for thee: for my strength is made perfect in weakness. Most gladly therefore will I rather glory in my infirmities, that the power of Christ may rest upon me.

16. Galatians 2:20
    I am crucified with Christ: nevertheless I live; yet not I, but Christ liveth in me: and the life which I now live in the flesh I live by the faith of the Son of God, who loved me, and gave himself for me.

17. Galatians 5:22–23
    But the fruit of the Spirit is love, joy, peace, longsuffering, gentleness, goodness, faith, Meekness, temperance: against such there is no law.

18. Philippians 4:13
    I can do all things through Christ which strengtheneth me.

19. Colossians 3:23
    And whatsoever ye do, do it heartily, as to the Lord, and not unto men.

20. Hebrews 12:1–2
    Wherefore seeing we also are compassed about with so great a cloud of witnesses, let us lay aside every weight, and the sin which doth so easily beset us, and let us

run with patience the race that is set before us, looking unto Jesus the author and finisher of our <u>faith</u>; who for the joy that was set before him endured the <u>cross</u>, despising the shame, and is set down at the right hand of the throne of God.

21. Hebrews 13:8
Jesus Christ the same <u>yesterday</u>, and to day, and for <u>ever</u>.

22. James 1:22
But be ye <u>doers</u> of the <u>word</u>, and not hearers only, deceiving your own <u>selves</u>.

23. James 4:7
<u>Submit</u> yourselves therefore to <u>God</u>. Resist the devil, and he will <u>flee</u> from you.

24. 2 Peter 3:9
The <u>Lord</u> is not slack concerning his <u>promise</u>, as some men count slackness; but is longsuffering to us-ward, not willing that any should <u>perish</u>, but that all should come to repentance.

25. 1 John 4:7–8
Beloved, let us <u>love</u> one another: for love is of God; and every one that loveth is born of God, and knoweth <u>God</u>. He that loveth not knoweth not God; for God is love.

48. Scriptures on Prayer

1. Psalm 19:14
Let the words of my <u>mouth</u>, and the meditation of my <u>heart</u>, be acceptable in thy sight, O Lord, my <u>strength</u>, and my redeemer.

2. Psalm 50:14–15
Offer unto God <u>thanksgiving</u>; and pay thy vows unto the most <u>High</u>: And call upon me in the day of trouble: I will deliver thee, and thou shalt <u>glorify</u> me.

3. Psalm 66:17
I cried unto him with my mouth, and he was extolled with my <u>tongue</u>.

4. Psalm 95:2
Let us come before his presence with <u>thanksgiving</u>, and make a joyful <u>noise</u> unto him with psalms.

5. Psalm 118:25
Save now, I beseech thee, O Lord: O Lord, I beseech thee, send now <u>prosperity</u>.

6. Psalm 119:11
Thy <u>word</u> have I hid in mine <u>heart</u>, that I might not <u>sin</u> against thee.

7. Psalm 119:105
Thy word is a <u>lamp</u> unto my <u>feet</u>, and a light unto my <u>path</u>.

8. Psalm 122:6
<u>Pray</u> for the <u>peace</u> of Jerusalem: they shall prosper that <u>love</u> thee.

9. Romans 10:1
Brethren, my heart's <u>desire</u> and <u>prayer</u> to God for Israel is, that they might be <u>saved</u>.

10. Romans 10:13
For <u>whosoever</u> shall call upon the <u>name</u> of the Lord shall be <u>saved</u>.

11. Romans 15:30
Now I beseech you, <u>brethren</u>, for the Lord <u>Jesus</u> Christ's sake, and for the <u>love</u> of the Spirit, that ye strive together with me in your <u>prayers</u> to God for me.

12. 1 Corinthians 1:4
I thank my God always on your <u>behalf</u>, for the <u>grace</u> of God which is given you by Jesus <u>Christ</u>.

13. 1 Corinthians 14:15
What is it then? I will pray with the <u>spirit</u>, and I will pray with the understanding also: I will sing with the spirit, and I will <u>sing</u> with the understanding also.

14. 2 Corinthians 1:11
Ye also helping together by <u>prayer</u> for us, that for the <u>gift</u> bestowed upon us by the means of many persons thanks may be given by many on our <u>behalf</u>.

15. Ephesians 6:18
<u>Praying</u> always with all prayer and <u>supplication</u> in the <u>Spirit</u>, and watching thereunto with all perseverance and supplication for all saints.

16. Philippians 1:3–4
I thank my <u>God</u> upon every <u>remembrance</u> of you, always in every <u>prayer</u> of mine for you all making request with joy.

17. Colossians 1:3
We give thanks to God and the Father of our Lord Jesus Christ, <u>praying</u> always for you.

18. 1 Thessalonians 5:17
<u>Pray</u> without ceasing.

19. 1 Thessalonians 5:18
In every thing give <u>thanks</u>: for this is the will of God in Christ Jesus concerning <u>you</u>.

20. James 1:6
But let him ask in <u>faith</u>, nothing wavering. For he that wavereth is like a wave of the <u>sea</u> driven with the wind and <u>tossed</u>.

21. James 5:13–14
Is any among you <u>afflicted</u>? let him <u>pray</u>. Is any merry? let him sing psalms. Is any sick among you? let him call for the elders of the <u>church</u>; and let them pray over him, anointing him with <u>oil</u> in the name of the Lord.

22. James 5:16
<u>Confess</u> your faults one to another, and <u>pray</u> one for another, that ye may be <u>healed</u>. The effectual fervent prayer of a righteous man availeth much.

49. Scriptures on Temptation

1. Matthew 6:13
And <u>lead</u> us not into <u>temptation</u>, but deliver us from evil: For thine is the kingdom, and the power, and the <u>glory</u>, for ever. Amen.

2. Matthew 26:41
Watch and <u>pray</u>, that ye enter not into <u>temptation</u>: the spirit indeed is willing, but the <u>flesh</u> is weak.

3. Luke 4:13
And when the <u>devil</u> had ended all the <u>temptation</u>, he departed from him for a <u>season</u>.

4. Luke 11:4
And <u>forgive</u> us our sins; for we also forgive every one that is <u>indebted</u> to us. And lead us not into <u>temptation</u>; but deliver us from evil.

5. Luke 22:40
And when he was at the <u>place</u>, he said unto them, <u>Pray</u> that ye enter not into temptation.

6. 1 Corinthians 7:2
Nevertheless, to <u>avoid</u> fornication, let every man have his own <u>wife</u>, and let every woman have her own <u>husband</u>.

7. 1 Corinthians 10:13
There hath no <u>temptation</u> taken you but such as is common to <u>man</u>: but God is <u>faithful</u>, who will not suffer you to be tempted above that ye are able; but will with the temptation also make a way to <u>escape</u>, that ye may be able to bear it.

8. 1 Timothy 6:9
But they that will be <u>rich</u> fall into temptation and a snare, and into many <u>foolish</u> and hurtful <u>lusts</u>, which drown men in destruction and perdition.

50. Scriptures on Hope

1. Numbers 23:19
God is not a <u>man</u>, that he should <u>lie</u>; neither the son of man, that he should repent: hath he said, and shall he not do it? or hath he spoken, and shall he not make it <u>good</u>?

2. Job 13:15
Though he <u>slay</u> me, yet will I <u>trust</u> in him: but I will maintain mine own <u>ways</u> before him.

3. Proverbs 24:14
So shall the knowledge of <u>wisdom</u> be unto thy <u>soul</u>: when thou hast found it, then there shall be a reward, and thy <u>expectation</u> shall not be cut off.

4. Proverbs 24:20
For there shall be no reward to the <u>evil</u> man; the candle of the <u>wicked</u> shall be put out.

5. Romans 8:24–25
For we are saved by <u>hope</u>: but hope that is seen is not <u>hope</u>: for what a man seeth, why doth he yet hope for? But if we hope for that we see not, then do we with <u>patience</u> wait for it.

6. 1 Corinthians 15:19
If in this <u>life</u> only we have hope in <u>Christ</u>, we are of all men most <u>miserable</u>.

7. Hebrews 11:1
Now <u>faith</u> is the substance of things <u>hoped</u> for, the evidence of <u>things</u> not seen.

8. 1 Peter 1:3
Blessed be the <u>God</u> and Father of our Lord Jesus <u>Christ</u>, which according to his abundant mercy hath begotten us again unto a lively hope by the <u>resurrection</u> of Jesus Christ from the <u>dead</u>.

51. Scriptures on Love

1. Leviticus 19:17–18
Thou shalt not hate thy <u>brother</u> in thine heart: thou shalt in any wise rebuke thy neighbour, and not suffer <u>sin</u> upon him. Thou shalt not avenge, nor bear any grudge against the <u>children</u> of thy people, but thou shalt <u>love</u> thy neighbour as thy-self: I am the LORD.

2. Psalm 30:5
For his <u>anger</u> endureth but a moment; in his favour is <u>life</u>: weeping may endure for a <u>night</u>, but joy cometh in the morning.

3. Psalm 103:8
The <u>LORD</u> is merciful and <u>gracious</u>, slow to anger, and plenteous in <u>mercy</u>.

4. Psalm 103:13
Like as a <u>father</u> pitieth his <u>children</u>, so the LORD pitieth them that fear <u>him</u>.

5. Psalm 143:8
Cause me to hear thy lovingkindness in the <u>morning</u>; for in thee do I trust: cause me to know the way wherein I should <u>walk</u>; for I lift up my soul unto thee.

6. Proverbs 10:12
<u>Hatred</u> stirreth up strifes: but <u>love</u> cov-ereth all sins.

7. Proverbs 21:21
He that followeth after <u>righteousness</u> and mercy findeth <u>life</u>, righteousness, and honour.

8. Isaiah 43:4
Since thou wast precious in my <u>sight</u>, thou hast been honourable, and I have loved <u>thee</u>: therefore will I give <u>men</u> for thee, and people for thy <u>life</u>.

9. Matthew 5:44
But I say unto you, <u>Love</u> your <u>enemies</u>, bless them that curse you, do good to them that hate you, and pray for them which despite-fully use you, and persecute <u>you</u>.

10. Mark 12:30
And thou shalt <u>love</u> the Lord thy God with all thy <u>heart</u>, and with all thy soul, and with all thy mind, and with all thy strength: this is the first <u>commandment</u>.

11. Mark 12:31
And the second is like, namely this, Thou shalt <u>love</u> thy neighbour as thyself. There is none other <u>commandment</u> greater than these.

12. Luke 10:27
And he answering said, <u>Thou</u> shalt love the Lord thy God with all thy <u>heart</u>, and with all thy <u>soul</u>, and with all thy strength, and with all thy mind; and thy neighbour as thyself.

13. John 14:21
He that hath my <u>commandments</u>, and keepeth them, he it is that <u>loveth</u> me: and he that loveth me shall be loved of my <u>Fa-ther</u>, and I will love him, and will manifest myself to him.

14. John 15:12
This is my <u>commandment</u>, That ye <u>love</u> one another, as I have <u>loved</u> you.

15. John 15:13
Greater love hath no <u>man</u> than this, that a man lay down his <u>life</u> for his <u>friends</u>.

16. Romans 8:38–39
For I am <u>persuaded</u>, that neither death, nor life, nor angels, nor principalities, nor <u>powers</u>, nor things present, nor things to come, Nor <u>height</u>, nor depth, nor any other creature, shall be able to separate us from the love of <u>God</u>, which is in Christ Jesus our Lord.

17. Romans 12:9
Let <u>love</u> be without dissimulation. Abhor that which is <u>evil</u>; cleave to that which is good.

18. Romans 12:10
Be kindly affectioned one to another with brotherly <u>love</u>; in honour preferring one another.

19. Romans 13:8
Owe no man any thing, but to <u>love</u> one another: for he that loveth another hath fulfilled the <u>law</u>.

20. Romans 13:10
<u>Love</u> worketh no <u>ill</u> to his neighbour: therefore love is the fulfilling of the law.

21. 1 Corinthians 2:9
But as it is <u>written</u>, Eye hath not seen, nor ear <u>heard</u>, neither have entered into the heart of man, the things which God hath prepared for them that <u>love</u> him.

22. 1 Corinthians 10:24
Let no <u>man</u> seek his own, but every man another's <u>wealth</u>.

23. 1 Corinthians 13:1
Though I speak with the <u>tongues</u> of men and of <u>angels</u>, and have not charity, I am become as sounding brass, or a tinkling <u>cymbal</u>.

24. 1 Corinthians 13:2
    And though I have the gift of <u>prophecy</u>, and understand all <u>mysteries</u>, and all knowledge; and though I have all faith, so that I could remove <u>mountains</u>, and have not charity, I am nothing.

25. 1 Corinthians 13:3
    And though I bestow all my <u>goods</u> to feed the poor, and though I give my <u>body</u> to be burned, and have not charity, it profiteth me <u>nothing</u>.

26. 1 Corinthians 13:4–5
    <u>Charity</u> suffereth long, and is kind; charity envieth not; charity vaunteth not itself, is not puffed up, doth not <u>behave</u> itself unseemly, seeketh not her own, is not easily provoked, thinketh no <u>evil</u>.

27. 1 Corinthians 16:14
    Let all your <u>things</u> be done with <u>charity</u>.

28. Ephesians 3:16–17
    That he would grant you, according to the <u>riches</u> of his <u>glory</u>, to be strengthened with might by his <u>Spirit</u> in the inner man; that Christ may dwell in your hearts by faith; that ye, being rooted and grounded in <u>love</u>.

29. Ephesians 4:2
    With all lowliness and <u>meekness</u>, with longsuffering, forbearing one another in <u>love</u>.

30. Ephesians 4:15
    But speaking the truth in <u>love</u>, may grow up into him in all <u>things</u>, which is the head, even <u>Christ</u>.

31. Ephesians 5:2
    And walk in love, as Christ also hath <u>loved</u> us, and hath given <u>himself</u> for us an offering and a sacrifice to <u>God</u> for a sweetsmelling savour.

32. Ephesians 5:25–26
    <u>Husbands</u>, love your <u>wives</u>, even as Christ also loved the church, and gave himself for it; That he might sanctify and cleanse it with the washing of water by the word.

33. Colossians 3:14
    And above all these things put on <u>charity</u>, which is the bond of <u>perfectness</u>.

34. 1 Thessalonians 3:12
    And the Lord make you to increase and abound in <u>love</u> one toward another, and toward all <u>men</u>, even as we do toward you.

35. 2 Thessalonians 3:5
    And the Lord direct your <u>hearts</u> into the love of God, and into the <u>patient</u> waiting for Christ.

36. 2 Timothy 1:7
    For God hath not given us the spirit of <u>fear</u>; but of power, and of love, and of a sound <u>mind</u>.

37. 1 Peter 4:8
    And above all things have fervent <u>charity</u> among yourselves: for charity shall cover the multitude of <u>sins</u>.

38. 1 John 3:1
    Behold, what manner of love the <u>Father</u> hath bestowed upon <u>us</u>, that we should be called the sons of God: therefore the world knoweth us not, because it knew him not.

39. 1 John 3:11
    For this is the message that ye heard from the <u>beginning</u>, that we should <u>love</u> one another.

40. 1 John 4:9
    In this was manifested the <u>love</u> of God toward us, because that God sent his only begotten Son into the <u>world</u>, that we might live through him.

41. 1 John 4:10
    Herein is <u>love</u>, not that we loved God, but that he loved us, and sent his <u>Son</u> to be the propitiation for our <u>sins</u>.

42. 1 John 4:12
    No man hath seen <u>God</u> at any time. If we love one another, God dwelleth in us, and his love is perfected in <u>us</u>.

43. 1 John 4:16
    And we have known and believed the <u>love</u> that God hath to us. God is <u>love</u>; and he that dwelleth in love dwelleth in God, and God in him.

44. 1 John 4:18
    There is no fear in love; but perfect <u>love</u> casteth out <u>fear</u>: because fear hath torment. He that feareth is not made perfect in <u>love</u>.

45. 1 John 4:20
    If a man say, I love God, and hateth his brother, he is a <u>liar</u>: for he that loveth not his <u>brother</u> whom he hath seen, how can he love God whom he hath not seen?

46. Revelation 3:19
    As many as I <u>love</u>, I rebuke and <u>chasten</u>: be zealous therefore, and repent.

52. Crossword Puzzle 1

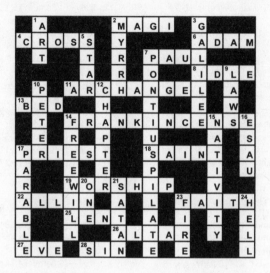

Section 2: The Intermediate Section

54. Group 1

1. True—(1 Chronicles 1:34)
2. False—Amnon was David's firstborn son (1 Chronicles 3:1)
3. False—Rehoboam was king after him (1 Chronicles 3:10)
4. False—Her hair is her glory (1 Corinthians 11:15)
5. True—(1 Corinthians 15:50)
6. True—(1 Corinthians 15:56)
7. True—(1 Corinthians 6:19)
8. False—He refers to himself as an apostle (1 Corinthians 9:1)
9. False—Solomon would be king (1 Kings 1:13)
10. False—He ruled for seventeen years (1 Kings 14:21)
11. True—(1 Kings 16:30–31)
12. True—(1 Kings 16:32)
13. False—Elijah performed the miracle (1 Kings 17:19–22)
14. True—(1 Kings 17:2–7)
15. False—He met the prophets of Baal on Mount Carmel (1 Kings 18:19)
16. True—(1 Kings 18:46)
17. False—He was fed two meals (1 Kings 19:5–8)
18. True—(1 Kings 19:8)
19. True—(1 Kings 19:8)
20. True—(1 Kings 4:26)

55. Group 2

1. False—Benaiah was the commander (1 Kings 4:4)
2. False—He was not allowed to build it (1 Kings 5:3)
3. False—He began to build in the fourth year of his reign (1 Kings 6:1)
4. True—(Ephesians 2:20)
5. True—(1 Peter 5:8)
6. True—(1 Samuel 1:9–20)
7. True—(1 Samuel 9:27; 10:1)
8. False—The head is usually anointed (1 Samuel 10:1)
9. True—(1 Samuel 13:8–14)
10. True—(1 Samuel 16:1, 13)
11. True—(1 Samuel 16:15–19)
12. False—He killed a bear and a lion (1 Samuel 17:34–36)
13. True—(Mark 10:46–52)
14. False—He was from Gath (1 Samuel 17:4)
15. True—(1 Samuel 17:4)
16. False—He took five stones (1 Samuel 17:40)
17. False—He used a slingshot and one stone (1 Samuel 17:49–50)
18. True—(1 Samuel 17:54)
19. True—(1 Samuel 18:11)
20. True—(1 Samuel 18:27)

56. Group 3

1. True—(1 Samuel 18:6–7)
2. True—(1 Samuel 2:18–21)
3. True—(1 Samuel 20:16–17)
4. False—He gave David Goliath's sword (1 Samuel 21:8–9)
5. False—He massacred eighty-five priests in the town of Nod (1 Samuel 22:18)
6. True—(1 Samuel 25:3)
7. True—(1 Samuel 28:8)
8. True—(1 Samuel 3:2–10)
9. False—His bones were buried under a tree (1 Samuel 31:12–13)
10. True—(1 Samuel 31:2)
11. True—(1 Samuel 31:3)
12. False—Three of his sons were killed (1 Samuel 31:8)
13. True—(1 Samuel 4:11)
14. True—(1 Samuel 4:4–5)
15. True—(1 Samuel 5:2)
16. True—(1 Samuel 7:17)
17. True—(1 Samuel 7:17)
18. True—(1 Samuel 9:1–2)
19. True—(1 Timothy 2:5)
20. False—Christians should lift up holy hands (1 Timothy 2:8)

57. Group 4

1. True—(2 Chronicles 13:21)
2. True—(2 Chronicles 17:11)
3. False—He saw the Lord sitting upon his throne (2 Chronicles 18:8–18)
4. True—(2 Chronicles 2:8)
5. True—(2 Chronicles 26:9–10)
6. True—(2 Chronicles 26:21)
7. False—Josiah disguised himself (2 Chronicles 35:20–22)
8. False—He was Hebrew by birth (Philippians 3:5)
9. True—(2 Corinthians 11:25)
10. False—Her name appears twice (2 Corinthians 11:3; 1 Timothy 2:13)
11. True—(2 Corinthians 1:1–2; 11:32–33)
12. True—(2 Corinthians 1:1–2; 12:2)
13. False—His bones brought a dead man back to life (2 Kings 13:20–21)
14. True—(2 Kings 2:11)
15. False—It divided (2 Kings 2:12–14)
16. False—He healed the waters of Jericho (2 Kings 2:18–22)
17. True—(Joshua 10:12–13; 2 Kings 20:8–11)
18. True—(2 Kings 22:1)
19. True—(2 Kings 23:29)
20. True—(2 Kings 25:1)

58. Group 5

1. False—Zedekiah was the last king (2 Kings 25:1–7)
2. True—(2 Kings 4:1–12)
3. False—He supplied oil (2 Kings 4:1–7)
4. True—(2 Kings 5:20–27)
5. True—(2 Kings 6:17)
6. True—(2 Kings 8:7–15)
7. True—(Jeremiah 26:20–23)
8. True—(2 Kings 9:31–33)
9. False—Dogs ate her body (2 Kings 9:35–37)
10. True—(2 Samuel 11:2–4)
11. True—(2 Samuel 12:1–15)
12. False—Solomon was their second son (2 Samuel 12:24)
13. True—(2 Samuel 12:24–25)
14. True—(2 Samuel 13:37–38)
15. False—He was handsome (2 Samuel 14:25)
16. True—(2 Samuel 15:30)
17. True—(2 Samuel 18:14–17)
18. True—(2 Samuel 2:4)
19. True—(2 Samuel 2:8–9)
20. False—He was also known as Eshbaal (1 Chronicles 9:39)

59. Group 6

1. True—(2 Samuel 20:15–22)
2. True—(2 Samuel 20:9–10)
3. True—(2 Samuel 21:12–14)
4. True—(2 Samuel 4:4)
5. True—(2 Samuel 4:6)
6. False—Jebusites inhabited Jerusalem (2 Samuel 5:6)
7. True—(2 Samuel 6:16)
8. False—Joab was the commander (2 Samuel 8:16)
9. False—His grandmother was Lois (2 Timothy 1:5)
10. False—His mother was Eunice (2 Timothy 1:5)
11. True—(2 Timothy 4:12)
12. False—There were only two soldiers (Acts 12:6)
13. True—(Acts 1:15–26)
14. True—(Acts 10:1–45)
15. True—(Acts 10:24–48)
16. False—They were first called Christians at the church of Antioch (Acts 11:26)
17. True—(Acts 11:27–28)
18. False—James the brother of John was the first (Acts 12:1–2)
19. True—(Acts 12:1–2)
20. True—(Acts 12:18–19)

60. Group 7

1. True—(Acts 12:23)
2. True—(Acts 12:6–17)
3. True—(Acts 13:13–14)
4. True—(Acts 13:9)
5. True—(Acts 14:8–19)
6. True—(Acts 15:32)
7. False—He was accompanied by Silas (Acts 15:40–41)
8. True—(Acts 16:14)
9. True—(Acts 16:14)
10. True—(Acts 16:14–15)
11. False—They were famous for searching the Scriptures (Acts 17:10–11)
12. True—(Acts 18:2)
13. True—(Acts 18:8)
14. True—(Acts 19:19)
15. False—It was in Ephesus (Acts 19:1–9)
16. False—Peter preached at Pentecost (Acts 2)
17. False—He was in Troas (Acts 20:6–9)
18. True—(Acts 9:36–43; 20:9–12)
19. True—(Acts 21:39)
20. True—(Acts 22:3)

61. Group 8

1. True—(Acts 22:3)
2. False—He came to report a conspiracy (Acts 23:16)
3. True—(Acts 23:20–21)
4. True—(Acts 24:1)
5. True—(Acts 24:27)
6. False—He left Paul bound in prison (Acts 24:27)
7. False—It was the name of a storm (Acts 27:14)
8. True—(Acts 28:3–6)
9. False—John and Peter healed a crippled man (Acts 3:1–10)
10. True—(Acts 4:36)
11. False—It means "the son of consolation" (Acts 4:36)
12. False—Joses was his original name (Acts 4:36)
13. False—About five thousand men believed (Acts 4:4)
14. False—A Pharisee was a doctor of the law (Acts 5:34)
15. True—(Acts 5:34)
16. True—(Acts 6:7–8:2)
17. True—(Acts 7:59)
18. False—The Spirit of the Lord carried him (Acts 8:39–40)
19. False—Simon the sorcerer tried to buy the gifts (Acts 8:9, 18–19)
20. False—Saul was headed to Damascus (Acts 9:1)

62. Group 9

1. False—He was healed by Peter (Acts 9:32–34)
2. False—Peter raised her from the dead (Acts 9:36–41)
3. True—(Acts 9:8)
4. False—He was a herdsman (Amos 1:1)
5. False—He spoke about justice rolling down like a river (Amos 5:24)
6. False—He told believers to set their affections on things above (Colossians 3:2)
7. False—He described him as a beloved physician (Colossians 4:14)
8. False—He was king of Babylon (Daniel 1:1)
9. False—It was Mishael (Daniel 1:7)
10. True—(Daniel 2:1)
11. True—(Daniel 2:6)
12. True—(Daniel 5)
13. False—King Darius was "the Mede" (Daniel 5:31)
14. True—(Daniel 6)
15. False—He prayed three times a day (Daniel 6:10)
16. True—(Daniel 6:18)
17. False—He had a vision of a lion with eagle's wings (Daniel 7:4)
18. True—(Daniel 8:15–26; 9:21–27)
19. False—He visited Daniel (Daniel 9:20)
20. False—He was 120 years old (Deuteronomy 34:7)

63. Group 10

1. True—(Deuteronomy 10:6)
2. True—(Deuteronomy 12:6)
3. True—(Deuteronomy 3:11)
4. True—(Deuteronomy 32:48–49)
5. True—(Deuteronomy 34:3)
6. True—(Deuteronomy 34:5–6)
7. False—They mourned for thirty days (Deuteronomy 34:8)
8. True—(Exodus 20:12; Deuteronomy 5:16)
9. True—(Deuteronomy 9:13)
10. True—(Ecclesiastes 2:2)
11. True—(Ephesians 5:14)
12. False—He recommended the Holy Spirit as a substitute for wine (Ephesians 5:18)
13. False—Hadassah was her Hebrew name (Esther 2:7)
14. True—(Esther 2:7)
15. False—He was angry because Mordecai wouldn't bow down to him (Esther 3:5)
16. True—(Esther 3:8–9)
17. False—Zeresh was his wife (Esther 5:10)
18. True—(Exodus 1:13)
19. True—(Exodus 10:16)
20. True—(Exodus 10:19)

64. Names of God Part 1

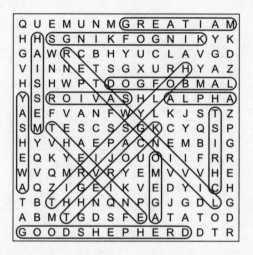

65. Names of God Part 2

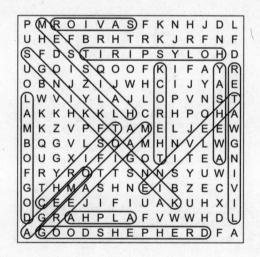

66. Names of God Part 3

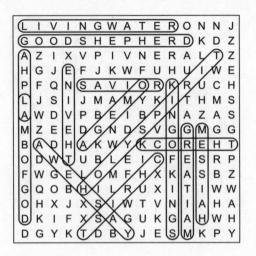

67. Abraham's Progeny Part 1

68. Abraham's Progeny Part 2

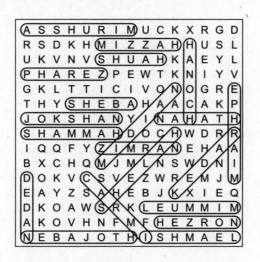

69. Abraham's Progeny Part 3

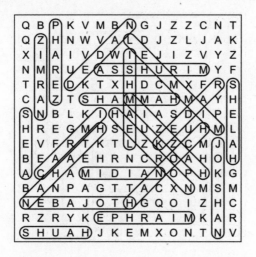

70. Women in the Bible Part 1

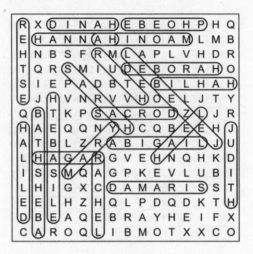

71. Women in the Bible Part 2

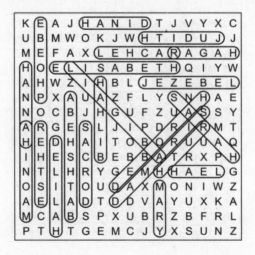

72. Women in the Bible Part 3

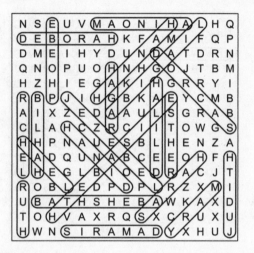

73. Prisoners and Exiles Part 1

74. Prisoners and Exiles Part 2

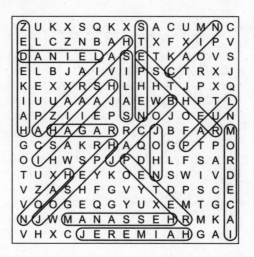

75. Prisoners and Exiles Part 3

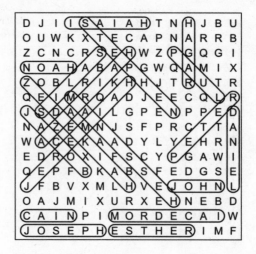

Section 3: The Bonus Section

76. Food by the Book

Dairy Products
1. Butter
2. Cheese
3. Butter
4. Eggs
5. Milk

Fruits
1. Apple
2. Date
3. Fig
4. Grape
5. Melon
6. Olive
7. Pomegranate
8. Raisin
9. Sycamore fruit

Vegetables
1. Cucumbers, leeks, and onions
2. Gourds

Nuts
1. Almonds
2. Pistachio nuts (NIV)

Legumes
1. Beans and lentils
2. Lentils

Spices and Herbs
1. Mint, anise, and cummin
2. Coriander
3. Cinnamon
4. Dill
5. Garlic
6. Mint
7. Mustard
8. Rue
9. Salt

Fish
1. Seven
2. Peter

Various Grains
1. Barley
2. Bread
3. Corn
4. Flour
5. Wheat, barley, millet, and spelt (a form of hardy wheat)

6. Unleavened bread
7. Wheat

Various Meats
1. Calf
2. Goat
3. Lamb
4. Oxen
5. Sheep
6. Venison

Various Fowl
1. Partridge
2. Pigeon
3. Quail
4. Dove

Miscellaneous
1. Grape juice
2. Honey
3. Olive oil
4. Vinegar
5. Wine

77. Crossword Puzzle 2

78. Crossword Puzzle 3

Timothy E. Parker is a Guinness World Records Puzzle Master, an ordained minister, and the editor of the Universal lines of puzzles. He is the author of more than thirty books. CNN calls his puzzles "Smart games for smart people," and he has created custom games for companies including Microsoft, Disney, Coca-Cola, Nike, Warner Bros., and Comcast.